Getting Rich in Late Antique Egypt

NEW TEXTS FROM ANCIENT CULTURES

Edited by

Traianos Gagos†
James G. Keenan, Loyola University of Chicago
Terry Wilfong, University of Michigan

Settling a Dispute: Toward a Legal Anthropology of Late Antique Egypt
by Traianos Gagos and Peter van Minnen

Women of Jeme: Lives in a Coptic Town in Late Antique Egypt
by T. G. Wilfong

Wine, Wealth, and the State in Late Antique Egypt: The House of Apion at Oxyrhynchus
by T. M. Hickey

New Literary Papyri from the Michigan Collection: Mythographic Lyric and a Catalogue of Poetic First Lines
by Cassandra Borges and C. Michael Sampson

Materia Magica: The Archaeology of Magic in Roman Egypt, Cyprus, and Spain
by Andrew T. Wilburn

Honor Among Thieves: Craftsmen, Merchants, and Associations in Roman and Late Roman Egypt
by Philip F. Venticinque

Getting Rich in Late Antique Egypt
by Ryan E. McConnell

Getting Rich in Late Antique Egypt

Ryan E. McConnell

UNIVERSITY OF MICHIGAN PRESS
ANN ARBOR

Published in the United States of America by the
University of Michigan Press
Printed and bound by CPI Group (UK) Ltd, Croydon, CR0 4YY

2020 2019 2018 2017 4 3 2 1

A CIP catalog record for this book is available from the British Library.

Library of Congress Cataloging-in-Publication data has been applied for.
ISBN 978-0-472-13038-2 (hardcover : alk. paper)
ISBN 978-0-472-12291-2 (e-book)

For Mom, Dad, Timmy, Chris, and Heather,
and all our families everywhere

Contents

Acknowledgments

My thanks are due, first, to Maryline Parca, for introducing me to the discipline of papyrology, for her constant guidance and careful feedback, and for pointing me in interesting and productive directions through many drafts and revisions of this book. I thank the organizers of the Summer Institute in Papyrology held at the University of Michigan in 2009—Jim Keenan, Arthur Verhoogt, Terry Wilfong, and especially the late Traianos Gagos—and my fellow participants, with whom I discovered a passion for puzzling over papyri. I am further grateful to Jim Keenan for his comments on early drafts of this book, which greatly improved the final product. Lajos Berkes, Giovanni Ruffini, Philip Venticinque, and Todd Hickey have my sincere appreciation for helpful conversations and correspondence about the book.

To my friends from the University of Illinois—Loula Strolonga, Dan Abosso, Amy Oh, Amy Norgard, Aine McVey, Sebastian Anderson, Jessie Wells, and especially Ingrid Albrecht—I owe my best memories of graduate school (and my twenties). Kirk Sanders' boundless enthusiasm and energy in everything he does will always inspire me. My friends and colleagues at Bowdoin College—Todd Berzon, Matt Botsch, and Jenny Baca—were indispensable for their advice, moral support, and carpool antics as I worked on the book. I thank Jessie Carroll for supporting me in too many ways to list. Last and most important, I thank my parents, Tim and Judy, and my siblings, Timmy, Chris, and Heather, for their love and encouragement as far back as I can remember and farther.

Some material in chapter 3, including the table, first appeared in my article "More Land, More Production, or More Taxes? Growth and the Apion Estate," *Bulletin of the American Society of Papyrologists* 53 (forthcoming).

CHAPTER 1

The Apions and Their Wealth

An ivory diptych now in Oviedo, Spain, commemorates the consular games of Apion II with his image. He is depicted as quite young in it, and the papyri show that he was perhaps only ten years old and no older than twenty at the time of his consulship in 539.[1] His early accession to such high office was not earned by his merits—he seems to have held no position before consul—but is instead a testament to his family's already significant wealth and prestige. In the sixth century, the Apion family had a mansion near the hippodrome in Constantinople, and the quarter of the city in which it sat was called τὰ Ἀππίωνος, very likely named after the family.[2] The many expenditures required of a consul for horse races, theatrical performances, and processions in which coins were tossed to spectators also imply the young Apion II's immense fortune.[3] By the end of his life some forty years later, Apion II was, by title at least, the most esteemed member of the senate.[4] In contrast, the earliest attested member of the family, Strategius I, was a *novus homo* locally prominent in 436 as a *dioiketes* administering imperial land in Oxyrhynchus, Egypt.[5] The move from elite status in provincial Oxyrhynchus to elite status in the entire empire was probably

1. Beaucamp 2001, 165–71; Hickey 2012, 14; Volbach 1976, no. 32. On the value of diptychs generally and of Apion II's specifically, see Eastmond 2010.
2. Sarris 2006, 86; Janin 1964, 311.
3. *CJ* 105.1 and 105.2 delineate these expenditures. The laws actually reduce the consular expenditures, which had escalated beyond a sustainable level and threatened the emperor's place as benefactor in chief. Still, the total expenditures were between one thousand and two thousand pounds of gold. See Bagnall et al. 1987, 10–12.
4. Hickey 2012, 14–16.
5. Hickey 2012, 8–9. On the imperial lands in Egypt, the *domus divina,* and the Apions' role in its administration, see Azzarello 2012.

a product of the reciprocally reinforcing effects of increasing wealth and status. But during the intervening century between Strategius I and Apion II, some activity generated a great deal of wealth for the family.[6] How the family increased its wealth and the role its agricultural holdings in Oxyrhynchus played in this endeavor are the subject investigated in this book. The Apions and their estate are particularly suited to such an examination, thanks to the family's appearance in literary sources and, even more so, to the many extant papyri relating to the family. The Apion dossier consists of more than three hundred published contracts, accounts, letters, receipts, and other texts, with many more documents waiting to be published.

Historiography

The historiography of large estates[7] in Byzantine Egypt, like that of the Apions', begins in earnest with E. R. Hardy's monograph on the Apion *oikos*.[8] Hardy describes a protofeudal institution in which semiservile tenants were tied to land increasingly concentrated in the hands of aristocratic elites. The appearance in the papyri of registered farmers (*enapographoi georgoi*, equated with the *coloni adscripticii* of the law codes), private prisons, and private military (*bucellarii*) and police forces (*riparii*) associated with estates is taken to signify both a loss of freedom for the peasantry and a usurpation of state authority by the aristocratic elite.[9] *Autopragia*, the collection and rendering of an estate's taxes by the estate itself (or of a village's taxes by the village itself), was further taken as emblematic of the increased self-sufficiency and usurpation of authority on the part of the estates.[10] By retrojecting onto Byzantine Egypt contemporary ideas about the economic fruits gained by the dissolution of the English manorial economy, Hardy reasons that the inverse had occurred in Byzantine Egypt, that the emergence of something akin to an autarkic manorial economy had led

6. On likely contributions of lucrative marriage and inheritance to the family's early enrichment and increasing status, see Gonis 2004.
7. The term *estate* should not be understood here to mean a single, large, contiguous holding. In the Egyptian context, the term usually refers to the patchwork collection of holdings owned by a single household.
8. Gelzer 1909, Rouillard 1928, and H. I. Bell's *P.Lond.* editions and 1917 article laid much of the groundwork for Hardy, but Hardy's dissertation, which became his 1931 book, was the first monograph examining the evidence in depth.
9. Hardy 1931, 54–72.
10. Hardy 1931, 54–58.

to economic decline.[11] In sum, Hardy sees the estates asserting for themselves rights that had been the province of the imperial government, most notably security and taxation. This led, on the one hand, to increased oppression of the peasant class and, on the other, to greater isolation of rural areas from city economies; that is, in Hardy's view, the large estates led to both social and economic decline in the Byzantine period. Much of the subsequent scholarship has disputed Hardy's notions.

Johnson and West reject the idea of an economic decline in Byzantine Egypt, largely because of the increased use of irrigation machinery in the period. More irrigation, they argue, would mean more arable land and, therefore, more produce than ever before.[12] To explain the effects of the estates in the agrarian economy, they look beyond Hardy's view of economic decline to the land reforms of the fourth century, which diminished the significance of the designation of crown land to the point that it disappeared from the record by the end of the century.[13] This onetime crown land fell to the peasants who had merely worked it before, making them *de facto* owners.[14] Johnson and West see some large estates emerging as land was becoming newly available for capital investment, but they suggest that historians attribute an outsized role to large estates, owing to more extensive surviving documentation and study. They argue that autonomous villages formed from the free peasant landowners provided a new economic foundation following the land reforms. Noting imperial legislation aimed at curbing the growth of large estates, Johnson and West take the later absence of such laws under Justinian as evidence that the "evil was ended."[15] Similarly, they see the emergent problem of patronage, wherein members of the imperial bureaucracy exchanged protection for control over property, as having been successfully curtailed by imperial legislation.[16] The absence of these laws in sixth-century legislation and the evidence for continued peasant prosperity suggest to them that the earlier legislation was essentially successful at sidelining large estates.

Johnson and West claim that Hardy's assertions about the social signifi-

---

11. Sarris 2006, 133.
12. Johnson and West 1949, 7–13.
13. Diocletian imposed a tax system based on the surface area of land. While he did not alter the categories of land, the distinctions became essentially irrelevant, disappearing from the sources by the end of the fourth century. See Johnson and West 1949, 19.
14. Johnson and West 1949, 18–23.
15. Johnson and West 1949, 18 n. 23.
16. Johnson and West 1949, 22. On patronage, see Bagnall 1993, 214–19.

cance of *autopragia* and the *coloni adscripticii* are unwarranted. They argue instead that the *adscripticii* were free tenants, registered on the estates strictly for the purpose of determining where they were to be taxed, and that *autopragia* and the designation of *coloni adscripticii* (*enapographoi georgoi* in the papyri) were simply fiscal arrangements.[17] They suggest that estate prisons, which Hardy sees as evidence of peasant servility, were likely used to detain and ransom the families of defaulters, rather than to control workers not engaged in labor.[18] In stark contrast to Hardy's bleak picture of peasant life, Johnson and West see the peasants of Egypt as flourishing socially and culturally in this period.[19]

Along the same lines as Johnson and West, Carrié argues that the estates were less important to the overall economy than one might suspect from the surviving evidence—that they were only one among a variety of methods of exploiting the land.[20] Carrié notes the difficulty of drawing conclusions about social conditions (e.g., servility versus freedom) from the legal sources discussing the *coloni adscripticii*, to whom Hardy attaches so much importance. The designation of *adscripticius*, Carrié says, arose out of Diocletian's legal reforms dealing with the fiscal needs of the empire. Among those needs was ensuring a stable tax income and harvest, both of which could be adversely affected by the movement of workers. Diocletian therefore attempted to restrict such movement by tying taxpayers to a particular location. In this way, the existing poll tax shifted to a system in which a community was liable for a certain sum, with each member paying a share of that sum.[21] Communities were associated with a particular locality, and the members of that community were registered for tax purposes in that locality, their *origo*. Such a locality might be a village or a city or, in the case of the *coloni adscripticii*, an *epoikion* associated with an estate. For this reason, Carrié argues, the *adscripticii* should not be seen as any more servile than other groups with a particular *origo* associated with their taxation, since most groups had such a fiscal association.[22] The fiscal, rather

17. Johnson and West 1949, 31.
18. Johnson and West 1949, 31.
19. Rémondon (1974) was the first to draw attention to the disparity between the narrative of a semiservile, socially oppressed peasantry and the papyrological evidence for peasants of middling wealth, acting as both lessors and lessees. The extent and details of the dealings of these sometimes prosperous peasants have been examined by Keenan (1980, 1984, 2007) and MacCoull (1988).
20. Carrié 1983, 229.
21. Carrié 1983, 217–18. Johnson and West (1949, 259–64) dispute the notion that this *capitatio* tax was in fact a poll tax.
22. Carrié 1983, 217.

than social, nature of the relationship is further highlighted by the fact that the state, not the landowner, designated the estate as the *origo*.[23]

Gascou advances this position further by claiming that the estates became semipublic institutions. In contrast to Hardy's assertions that the estates usurped state authority, Gascou argues that the state co-opted the private bureaucratic apparatus of estates (employed for the purposes of collecting dues and produce, distributing payments and supplies, etc.) for a number of functions.[24] By the fifth and sixth centuries, Gascou asserts, the estates had become the organizational focal point for the division of duties, responsible not only for their own taxes but also for the collection of taxes from those near the estates.[25] The way in which the large estates were organized by their aristocratic owners (often themselves members of the imperial bureaucracy) could readily be exploited for official purposes. Hence the contributions noted for a particular household were actually the contributions of that household and all those from whom the household collected.[26] The estates, in turn, were organized into collectives, *syntelestai*, among whose members various duties were delegated.[27] This scheme has become known as the *fiscal participation model.* Under this model, both taxes and rent were paid to the same people, so the distinction between rent and tax began to disappear. Gascou presses this point further, arguing that public land was handed over to private individuals on emphyteutic leases, that is, on permanent leases of state or church land with an upfront payment and low annual payments.[28] Such annual payments to the government for productive land were indistin-

23. Carrié 1983, 218.

24. Similarly, Rémondon (1974), like Carrié, sees *autopragia* as imperially sanctioned by the time of the Apions. Rémondon argues that *autopragia* began as a privilege bestowed on certain estates by imperial authorities but that estates began to assert the privilege for themselves. In response, authorities made attempts to curtail the practice but ultimately tolerated and then recognized it. By recognizing the right, imperial authorities used the private structures to carry out official business. Rémondon explains the *bucellarii* and *riparii* as similarly disposed, as private groups employed for government purposes.

25. Gascou 1985, reprinted as Gascou 2008, 125–213, with a brief preface but otherwise unchanged.

26. In the past, this has led, as Hickey (2012, 153–54) has pointed out, to a great overestimation of the amount of land comprising an estate like the Apions'.

27. Liebeschuetz (1996, 395–401), who is skeptical of Gascou's case for such formal collectives on the absence of evidence for a robust legal vocabulary to describe the arrangement, emphasizes the irregular nature of any such arrangement, which is attractive for the model laid out in the present work. Laniado (1996) is also dubious of giving *syntelestes* any definition grander than "taxpayer." See, however, the epilogue to Zuckerman 2004, 238–40.

28. Johnson and West 1949, 72–74. Gascou's identification of apotactic—i.e., invariable—payments with emphyteutic leases is one of the more controversial aspects of his model. For discussion, see Sarris, 2006, 155–56; Banaji 2001, 94–94; Hickey 2012, 53–58.

guishable from taxes paid on owned land, hence Gascou's designation of them as *rentes-impôts*.[29] In sum, the public responsibilities that had before fallen to the civic *curia* fell to the estates, and rents, indistinguishable from taxes, ended up in government coffers.[30] A key difference between Gascou's model and those of Carrié and Johnson and West is therefore the centrality of the large estate. As Sarris has commented, "In this sense at least, the Gascou thesis is closer in spirit to the work of Hardy than might be supposed."[31]

While largely agreeing with Gascou's fiscal participation model, Bagnall has pointed out a fundamental problem with the contention that estates were public institutions: "The documentation . . . includes some transactions comprehensible only in the context of a private economy. And clearly the public role was only possible if substantial private wealth remained to sustain the whole enterprise."[32] Hickey seeks to address this shortcoming in Gascou's model by examining the private economy of the Apion estate, essential to its public functions. He determines that viticulture is the most likely candidate for producing a marketable surplus.[33] In the course of his investigation, Hickey finds that the amount of land devoted to vineyards was surprisingly small on the Apion estate. This discovery has two main implications.

First, given the percentage of lands usually devoted to vineyards, the small amount of vineyard land implies that the Apion holdings were much smaller than had hitherto been estimated.[34] Hickey offers a revised figure that accords better with the expected ratio of vineyard land to total land. The smaller figure for the area of the estate appears to be at odds with the papyri recording the Apions' large contribution to the *annona civica* (e.g., *P.Oxy.* 1.127); such a large contribution could only be produced by a much greater area of land (and was the basis for earlier estimates of the size of the estates). But this discrepancy is readily explained by Gascou's model: the *annona civica* contributions documented in the papyri include the contributions not only of the Apion estate but also of other smaller producers from whom the Apions collected. Hickey's interpretation of the evidence again supports the idea that the Apions assumed

29. Under Gascou's model, the duties of the *bucellarii* and *riparii* are simply another example, along with tax collection, of the delegation of state power to the estates.
30. Evidence of the degree to which public and private had merged with the advent of the fiscal participation model can be seen, according to Gascou (1985, 19), in the increasing prevalence of official language used in ostensibly private contexts.
31. Sarris 2006, 141.
32. Bagnall 1993, 160.
33. Hickey 2012, chapters 1–3.
34. Hickey 2012, 153–54.

the bureaucratic and administrative roles that had once been held by the civic *curia*. Moreover, the evidence for smaller estates fractures a cornerstone of the feudal model, which entails large estates managed directly.[35]

Second, the small area devoted to vineyards indicates that the Apion estate was not particularly interested in producing a marketable surplus from which to derive profit. Hickey examines several agricultural sectors on the Apion estate and fails to find indicators of profit-seeking behavior. Rathbone demonstrates that accounts from the third-century Heroninus archive dealing with the Appianus estate reveal centrally directed management geared toward producing a marketable surplus.[36] He cautions, however, against projecting the same level of rationalism in management into the sixth century and to estates like the Apions'.[37] With findings concerning crop selection, market engagement, and levels of risk aversion in the Apions' undertakings, Hickey affirms Rathbone's caution in attributing the rationalism of the Appianus estate to that of the Apions: the Apion estate did not privilege crops with a potential for a marketable surplus, and the estate was essentially autarkic and risk averse.[38]

Banaji's study of late antique estates arrives at very different conclusions about rationalism in the sixth century. Rejecting notions of decline in the late antique economy, Banaji argues instead for economic prosperity and an increase in rural population, leading to an active labor market. The prosperity, Banaji argues, is linked to the establishment in the fourth century of a stable currency based on the intrinsic value of gold. Because its value was so stable, gold became the preferred investment for storing wealth. Government officials, therefore, favored payment in gold, which led to a preference for taxes collected in gold rather than in kind. Through successful investment in gold, a new class of wealthy landowners who became the main power brokers emerged. For Banaji, the change had two major implications: first, the rural economy must have been highly monetized for producers to pay taxes in coin, which implies a high level of market engagement on the part of farmers; second, a stable wealth base allowed aristocrats to invest in

35. On Sarris' formulation (2006, 198), larger estates "seem to have been conducive to . . . the more widespread introduction of direct forms of estate management, bipartite estates better suited to specialised production for the market."

36. These accounts reveal a highly monetized economy with fairly advanced accounting systems concerned with minimizing production costs by monitoring the efficiency of the overseers of different parts of the estate.

37. Rathbone 1991, 402–3. Rathbone's chief concern is that the incredible inflation at the end of the third century would have made the type of accounting found in the Appianus estate accounts untenable for the later centuries.

38. Hickey 2012.

agriculture, especially in the potentially profitable sector of viticulture.[39] Banaji's findings lead him to reevaluate the feudalistic view that absentee landowners derived steady income from tied *coloni* who rented the privilege to work the land. Instead, Banaji describes landowners actively engaged in the management of estates directed toward meeting the demands of the urban market, which he claims were extensive. Crucial to this management was control over the mobility and deployment of labor. This, Banaji claims, explains the numerous legal and contractual mechanisms by which landowners controlled workers, who mainly worked for a wage rather than renting.

In his examination of the extant accounts of the Apion estate, Sarris finds evidence for specialization, central direction, bureaucratic hierarchy, monetization, and accountability of overseers. All of these mechanisms, Sarris argues (in the same vein as Banaji), indicate that the estates were sophisticated, rationally managed enterprises, directed toward meeting the needs of urban markets. Sarris proposes a bipartite model of the estates, in which certain portions of the estate's lands were rented out and certain portions were directly managed using wage labor. He argues that the accounts demonstrate that the directly managed portion (the *autourgia*) provided the bulk of the marketable surplus for the estates, while the leased portions (the *ktemata*) yielded a more modest production intended to meet the needs of the *autourgia*. In addition to meeting the *autourgia*'s needs for produce, the lessees of ktematic land were drawn on to work the *autourgia* during harvest and sowing. In the accounts, names of people appear along with the names of the land they cultivated. The *origines* of these cultivators are also recorded, and the land cultivated and the *origo* are often the same. Some of the cultivated land, however, differs from the *origo* of the cultivator working it. Sarris interprets this evidence to indicate that labor was deliberately transferred between properties to meet the particular needs of different areas at different times, indicating central direction in the management of the estate.[40] Furthermore, certain *epoikia*—usually translated as "hamlets"[41] but described by Sarris as "labour settlements" for the *autourgia*[42]—show some signs of agricultural specialization, another indication of central direction and "tactical management."[43]

39. Banaji therefore harkens back to Johnson and West's earlier linking of irrigation and prosperity.
40. Sarris 2006, 36–39.
41. E.g., Bagnall 1993, 151.
42. Sarris 2006, 36–39.
43. Sarris 2006, 197–98.

Sarris also sees in the accounts a highly complex bureaucracy guiding proceeds from agricultural surplus upward. There is direct evidence for levels of administration, from the *phrontistai* (who oversaw the *ktemata*), to offices in Oxyrhynchus, and on to Alexandria and probably to Constantinople. Accounts from lower levels were collated, and sums were converted to different standards of currency at higher levels, with various levies extracted along the way. The activities of these administrators, as recorded in the accounts, mark not only the sophistication of the bureaucracy but also the highly monetized nature of the rural economy. Sarris argues that because demand was relatively stable, cost reduction was the most reliable means of increasing profit margins. The purpose of the accounts, therefore, was to ensure the "honesty and reliability" of the overseers, to make them accountable to the next administrative rung for any unusual outlays or shortfalls.[44] In arguing that such cost control demonstrates rational management, Sarris quotes Rathbone's conclusions about the accounts of the Heroninus archive: "The interest . . . in rigorous control of its costs of production . . . in itself indicates a high level of economic rationality in its management."[45]

The conclusions that Banaji and Sarris draw from their analyses push back against Gascou's model and Hickey's conclusions. Banaji's primary objections concern Gascou's equation of the land classed as ὑπὲρ ἀποτάκτου χωρίων (which appears frequently in the Apion accounts) with emphyteutic leases;[46] his claim that the distinction between rents and taxes dissolved; and the emphasis on the public (rather than private) control over estate labor.[47] Sarris, who envisions a "bitter struggle between the imperial authorities and aristocratic interests over access to the wealth created by—and extractable from—the labouring population of the empire,"[48] argues that Gascou's failure to apprehend the significance of the *autourgia* severely undermines his overall argument about the semipublic status of the estates.[49] Sarris, like Banaji, objects further to Gascou's identification of emphyteutic leases in the Apion archive and points to an absence of evidence, papyrological or legal, for the

44. Sarris 2006, 146.
45. Sarris 2006, 145.
46. Not accepting this aspect of Gascou's argument, Hickey (2012, 53–58) argues that emphyteutic leases were only one type of apotaktic (or fixed-rent) lease. He further connects land ὑπὲρ ἀποτάκτου χωρίων with vineyard land.
47. Banaji 2001, 93–100.
48. Sarris 2006, 7.
49. Sarris 2006, 155.

diminution of civic structures or for the formal colleges of aristocrats that Gascou claims replaced them.[50]

Ruffini's dissertation and the book it became use prosopographical connections and social network analysis to examine life in sixth-century Oxyrhynchus and Aphrodito.[51] Given the nature of the evidence, his examination of Oxyrhynchus necessarily focuses on the Apions. He finds a "highly centralized aristocratic elite whose economic power grew in relative isolation from social ties."[52] Society in sixth-century Oxyrhynchus, he argues, had a hierarchical structure, with the Apion family and the estate at the top. His conclusions about Oxyrhynchus contrast sharply with those about Aphrodito, which he describes as "a village society built on strong multiplex ties, a society in which economic action took place on social lines, a decentralized society in which literacy and mobility could give social prominence to men and women of relatively low social standing."[53] These findings appear to support the traditional views of these two locales, but Ruffini argues for a new explanation for these differences. Rather than reverting back to tired notions of *Sonderstellung* (which have dogged historical papyrological studies) or supposing that the incomplete evidence provides only a partial picture of both places,[54] he claims that the difference reflects differences in scale, with Oxyrhynchus providing the nome-level perspective, Aphrodito the village-level one.[55] The notion that qualitatively different economic activities occur at different levels of society—peasant, collector, aristocrat—is fundamental to the present work.

Central Question

The current *status quaestionis* regarding the large estates of Byzantine Egypt revolves chiefly around the level of market engagement on the Apion estate. Sarris and Hickey are the exponents of each side of the debate, arguing for high and low levels of market engagement, respectively. Sarris has suggested that

50. Sarris 2006, 155–57.
51. Ruffini 2005, 2008.
52. Ruffini 2008, 3.
53. Ruffini 2008, 3.
54. Zuckerman (2004, especially 221–22) claims to have identified a large estate in Aphrodito similar to the Apions' in Oxyrhynchus, though the evidence is tenuous. See Keenan 2005 (a review of Zuckerman 2004).
55. Ruffini 2008, 2–3.

unlike other categories of land, which were leased out, the *autourgia*, occasionally referenced in the accounts and elsewhere, was directly managed by the estate, with its substantial surpluses sold for the profit of estate owners. The surpluses from the *autourgia* do not appear in extant accounts, because, Sarris asserts, they would have been kept in accounts separate from leased lands, the *ktemata*. Alternatively, Hickey identifies the agricultural sectors that offered the greatest potential for profits, including especially wine production, and finds little emphasis on those sectors in the extant papyri. This implies that little profit was derived from the goods produced on the estates. If the *autourgia* was not a significant source of wealth and if Hickey accurately characterizes the estates as autarkic, the Apions must have drawn on another source of wealth.[56] I posit that the Apions' role in tax collection on behalf of the state was a significant source of the family's wealth.

The models of the Apion estate that are presented by Sarris and Hickey also offer strongly contrasting visions of its relationship with the state. Indeed, the evidence can point sometimes toward antagonism and sometimes toward a coziness. A third approach, offered here as something of a by-product of the explanation for Apion wealth, can accommodate both types of evidence by envisioning the relationship as closer to parties in a negotiation than to either patronage or eristic grasping.

In chapter 2, I argue, *pace* Sarris, that the *autourgia* did not produce a large surplus but, instead, was devoted to fodder production for a centralized transportation and animal infrastructure. Chapter 3 describes the Apion estate as operating on a two-tiered system and details the lower tier. The estate drew money upward from its collection agents through contractual arrangements meant to skim some of the money from collectors' speculation. The structure of the lower tier can also explain how a monetary economy could exist, absent direct market engagement by the estate. Comparing accounts from the lower tier to those from the upper tier also indicates that the amount of land over which the Apions had collection responsibility expanded rapidly in the sixth century. Chapter 4 argues that the relationship between the upper tier of the Apion estate and the state is difficult to ascertain directly, but scholarship examining historical methods of tax collection in a variety of milieus can limit the possibilities. Which of these possibilities was employed by a state is determined

56. Hickey (2012, 155) suggests imperial patronage as a possibility but does not elaborate further. On the relationship between consuls and the emperor at this time, see Bagnall et al. 1987, 10–12.

by sets of identifiable economic and environmental circumstances. The circumstances present in Byzantine Egypt suggest that a rent system, commonly known as tax farming, was the most likely arrangement between the Apions and the estate. Chapter 5 offers a comparative look at historical analogues for the two-tiered, large-scale, tax-farming system posited for the Apions.

Sources and Methods

The source material mined in investigating these issues consists primarily of papyrus accounts, contracts, letters, and leases. These documents date principally from the Byzantine period but also from the late Roman period, during which nascent versions of Byzantine social and economic structures can be seen. The Apion documents from Oxyrhynchus, as the richest source about a single estate spanning a large period of time, are central. The agricultural accounts are especially useful because they can offer material for quantitative evaluations of the estate's production over time and across space. The layout and purpose of these accounts, however, can often be opaque to the modern eye. These accounts are examined closely in chapters 2 and 3, and I would also direct readers to the edition of *P.Oxy.* 55.3804, a meticulously detailed explication of one of the best examples of these accounts. Chapter 3 examines how these accounts should be understood synoptically within the larger system in place for the Apion estate, by comparing them to accounts from a higher level of Apion administration. Despite the extensive number of documents from this period that inform us about estates in Oxyrhynchus, large gaps, of course, remain. Chapter 5 turns to a comparative method to help fill in these gaps. To this end, estates and methods of tax collection from other places and times with special relevance are discussed in relation to the Apion estate. Particularly useful also are legal sources, especially the laws of Justinian.

The Apions and the Archive

Getting a handle on the genealogy of the Apion family is often complicated by ancient and modern conventions of naming. Members in several generations of the family share the names *Apion* and *Strategius*, and modern scholarship uses Roman numerals to distinguish one from another. The emergence of new members in newly published documents can confuse the situation. For example, after the publication of *P.Oxy.* 50.4584–86, the family member identified in earlier scholarship as Strategius I became Strategius II. Mazza's 2001 monograph organizes the evidence about the Apion family and the archive into an accessible format, disentangling these issues and tracking the careers and connections of members of the family. Her work also lists the papyri associated with the archive (to the date of her book's publication) and includes very useful appendixes gathering place-names, sizes, archaeological provenance, and other information about the locations mentioned in documents in the archive.

CHAPTER 2

Reconsidering the *Autourgia*

An incomplete papyrological record may explain the discrepancy between the rising level of wealth attained by the Apions from the early fifth through the late seventh centuries and the lack of evidence for a clear means by which they acquired that wealth. The record can be incomplete in two broad ways. First, the picture of Oxyrhynchus that the papyri provide may be accurate, but Oxyrhynchus may be an outlier among the Apion holdings; that is, Apion holdings and other similar estates in other areas of Egypt might have been structured differently than they were in Oxyrhynchus[1] and might have produced massive surpluses to be sold at market for a profit. There is little that can be offered to rule out this possibility: comparisons to similar Byzantine estates elsewhere falter against a lack of evidence from other locales, and profound changes to the social and economic life in Egypt over the centuries make diachronic comparisons to large estates of earlier or later periods of limited use. In Aphrodito, the papyri evidence favors prosperous peasants rather than large landholders and provides an interesting contrast to the Oxyrhynchus documents.[2] For instance, Keenan has described the social and economic mobility of the peasant Aurelius Phoibammon, and Ruffini has found evidence of similar mobility in the social networks of the village.[3] But the social stratum usually described in the Aphro-

1. The noted scarcity of leases from the Oxyrhynchite compared to other Egyptian locales in the Byzantine period is a possible indicator of this, but see the section titled "Labor and Leasing Arrangements" below.
2. While Zuckerman (2004, especially chapters 1 and 4) has sought to find evidence of an Apion-like estate in Aphrodito, the results are tenuous. See also Keenan 2005 (a review of Zuckerman 2004).
3. In his 2007 essay, Keenan revises his 1980 assessment of Phoibammon's career, seeing him as a highly prosperous farmer rather than as an ascending peasant in the Horatio Alger mold. See Ruffini 2008.

dito documents is so different from that described in the Apion documents that direct comparanda are hard to find. Isolated pieces of evidence found here and there can illuminate contemporary estates elsewhere in Egypt (e.g., in the Fayyum),[4] but even when glimpses are caught, they differ in quality and quantity from the documentation for the Apion estates.[5] Broader conclusions drawn from any investigation into the topic of Byzantine estates in Egypt that relies on the Apion papyri must therefore be somewhat circumscribed. Apion evidence may apply elsewhere, but the possibility that Oxyrhynchus is an outlier must be borne in mind when conclusions drawn from it are applied elsewhere.

Second, the papyrological record may be incomplete owing to the inconsistent survival of different types of documents, distorting the impression of Oxyrhynchus. The argument goes that more weight than warranted has been given to certain types of documents from the estate, only because they survived while equally significant documents were lost. Scholars have long been concerned that the hazards of survival have unduly skewed perceptions of the Apion estate. Johnson and West, Carrié, and Rémondon have all raised the issue.[6] Peter Sarris' 2006 monograph, *Economy and Society in the Age of Justinian*, takes this evidentiary bias as its premise. Sarris offers the most fully fleshed out and forcefully argued examination of the Apion estate since Gascou's 1985 article.[7] Sarris proposes a bipartite model of the Apion estate, in which certain portions of the estate's lands were leased out while certain portions were directly managed using wage labor. The directly managed portions of the estates provided the bulk of the marketable surplus for the estates, and the leased portions, the *ktemata*, produced a more modest yield. Sarris identifies the directly managed portion of the estates with a category of land called the *autourgia*, which appears occasionally in the accounts and a handful of other documents. Because the accounts that have survived show only the income and expenditures of the ktematic land and not what is taken to be the

4. The sixth-century archive of Sambas *elaiourgos*, consisting of about thirty documents, contains orders for delivery of oil as payment to various groups on behalf of a Fayyum estate. Payments are to artisans and *buccellarii*, so the archive can help answer questions raised by the Apion documents from Oxyrhynchus, but it is not rich or varied enough to bolster broad conclusions about the functioning of the estates as a whole.

5. Ruffini (2008, 246 and n. 6) and Bagnall have borrowed the physics term *dark matter* to describe the problem: there are aspects of life in Aphrodito or Oxyrhynchus that we know must have existed but that we simply have no means of accessing.

6. See the section titled "Historiography" in chapter 1.

7. Hickey's 2001 dissertation and 2012 monograph are more narrowly focused than Sarris' holistic approach.

economically more significant autourgic land, studies treating these accounts as generally representative of the estates rely on a grossly distorted picture of how estates were actually organized.

Sarris' model has gained traction since its initial formulation and his subsequent publications on it, in many ways emerging as a dominant model in recent scholarship, especially outside of papyrology.[8] Whereas those earlier scholars who raised concerns about the representativeness of the Apion dossier mainly advised caution in the face of evidentiary gaps, Sarris seeks to fill in the lacunae, by mining the extant texts for clues about what is missing.[9] Inevitably, broad conclusions are drawn from scant evidence. This in itself is not necessarily a fault: seeing the microcosm in meager remains is often the work of a papyrologist, and finding a suitable set of meager remains in which it is possible to see the microcosm is, as Keenan writes, "every papyrological historian's dream."[10] Because of their wide scope and originality, any discussion of the Apions and the economy of Byzantine Egypt must stake out positions on Sarris' claims. His readings of the evidence are often highly original and built on each other, so it is necessary to reckon essentially with his model as a whole in order to reckon with any single claim. The bulk of this chapter is therefore devoted to an analysis and interrogation of Sarris' readings of key texts and to a revision of the conclusions he draws from them. The main areas to be discussed are how the *autourgia* is identified in the papyri, the nature of leasing and labor arrangements, whether the estates can be seen as expanding over time, the nature of production on the *autourgia*, and the role of the *autourgia* on the estates. The remaining chapters turn to a positive model of the estate's economy.

Identifying the Autourgia *in the Papyri*

Claiming that the *autourgia* appears in the expenditures portions of the extant accounts but not in the income portion, Sarris concludes that production on the *ktemata* supported the needs of the *autourgia*. Those needs were not only for material but also for labor, so tenants from the *ktemata* were obliged to work

8. See reviews by Bjornlie (2007) and Maas (2008). See also Whittow 2009. Mayerson (2006, 110 and n. 7), citing Sarris, describes Gascou's model of the Apion estates as "largely discredited."
9. See especially Sarris' use of historical analogy to fill the lacunae in his 2011 article.
10. Keenan 2005, 286 (in a review of Zuckerman 2004).

on the *autourgia* during times of the year when extra labor was needed.[11] This was essentially service labor, used for seasonal tasks such as planting and harvesting.[12] On Sarris' formulation, the estate-owned *epoikia*, or hamlets, around which the ktematic lands were situated, were labor settlements.[13] Through contracts or customary arrangements, the estates would oblige the inhabitants of these *epoikia* to work on the *autourgia* in exchange for housing, some provisioning, and access to land for leasing. On this model, the *autourgia* was the primary source of surpluses on the Apion estates, and these surpluses were sold at urban markets for a profit,[14] thereby explaining the wealth and prominence of the Apion family and why the extant accounts, concerned as they are with ktematic land, do not show significant surpluses. Presumably the estates kept accounts for autourgic land, like those extant for the ktematic lands, showing the great surpluses, but these accounts do not survive, remain undiscovered, or lie unedited. Sarris' position therefore argues from the assumption of severely incomplete sources. As a result, much of his work involves perusing surviving sources for evidence about production on the *autourgia* and the importance of this production.

The nature of the *autourgia*, however, is far from a settled issue. Most of the documents referring to the *autourgia* are not clear about what the term means or how the land it refers to was used. It is most often connected with land devoted to fodder.[15] Based on his reading of the papyri, however, Sarris argues that the *autourgia* was highly commercialized and geared toward producing a surplus of a number of different cash crops, not solely or even primarily fodder. Yet even if the *autourgia* was limited to the production of fodder, Sarris points out, landowners in later seigniorial economies sought to control meadows and other types of land where fodder grew. In such economies, this land was highly prized and kept under direct control, since its produce was essential to the productivity of land devoted to other types of crops and, as such, could be sold for profit. This explanation, however, does not account for the purchase of fodder and seed evidenced in Apion papyri.[16]

11. This point is reiterated throughout Sarris 2006. It is summarized at Sarris 2011, 265–66.
12. Sarris 2011, 267. Sarris (266) describes another system of direct management for those crops that required a steady input of labor, such as grapes, olives, and honey: certain persons or groups were assigned land to be worked and a production goal to be met in exchange for wages *in specie*.
13. Sarris 2006, 42.
14. Sarris 2011, 271–79.
15. On this connection and for references, see Mazza 2008, 152.
16. Sarris 2011, 268. On the purchase of fodder, see *P.Oxy.* 16.1911.178–80, 16.1913.36–39, 18.2195.132, 55.3804.244–48. See also Hickey 2001, 192–94 and n. 232.

Sarris offers *P.Oxy.* 16.1911 and 16.1913, annual accounts of estate stewards called *pronoetai*,[17] as evidence that the *autourgia* was productive of more than just fodder. His argument relies on two idiosyncratic readings of the text: (1) the meaning of the phrase ἔξω τῆς πύλης and its connection with the *autourgia* in the accounts and (2) the meaning of the term γεωργός. Sarris cites examples in *P.Oxy.* 16.1913 of vinedressers, garden farmers, and "land laborers" (*georgoi*) working on the *autourgia*.[18] He identifies the land in question as *autourgia* chiefly because it is called ἔξω τῆς πύλης, "Outside the Gate." Indeed, in *P.Oxy.* 16.1911 and 55.3804, the *autourgia* is named αὐτουργία ἔξω τῆς πύλης. In *P.Oxy.* 16.1913, however, the text says simply γεωργοὶ ἔξω τῆς πύλης, without mention of the *autourgia* or any other category of land. The Apions owned a large house referred to in the papyri as προάστιον ἔξω τῆς πύλης.[19] This house is known to have had several orchards,[20] and *P.Oxy.* 16.1911 and 55.3804 make it clear that *autourgia* land was associated with it. Such an association cannot, however, be inferred on the basis that αὐτουργία ἔξω τῆς πύλης is meant wherever the phrase ἔξω τῆς πύλης is used without qualification.[21] That the land category is only sometimes specifically called *autourgia* suggests that some distinction is being drawn when αὐτουργία is or is not appended to ἔξω τῆς πύλης.[22] If evidence for production on the *autourgia* is limited to texts mentioning that type of land explicitly, there is nothing to indicate that a variety of cash crops was grown on it.

Sarris' reading of *P.Oxy.* 16.1913 and other documents as relating to the *autourgia* also puts significant weight on the meaning of the word *georgos*. He construes it as meaning specifically and exclusively "land laborer" and understands this worker to be employed on the *autourgia*: "The *georgos* was obliged to reside on the *ktema*, provide general labour services on the *autourgia*, and pay his taxes."[23] *P.Oxy.* 1.135, on which Sarris relies in describing the terms of a *georgos*'

17. These accounts are discussed in detail in chapter 3.
18. Sarris 2011, 269–70.
19. *P.Oxy.* 16.1925; *PSI* 3.193; *P.Wisc.* 2.66.
20. Hickey 2012, 40 n. 6; Mazza 2001, 85–86.
21. See Hickey 2008, 97 n. 45. Hickey (2012, 150 n. 26) suggests that Sarris was misled by the translation of τῆς γεουχικ(ῆς) αὐτουργί(ας) Ἔξω τῆς Πύλης as "the landlord's *auturgia* (called) Outside the Gate," in the *editio princeps* of *P.Oxy.* 55.3804.269. The phrase might better be translated as "the landlords *autourgia* at the place called Outside the Gate." But the identification of all land Ἔξω τῆς Πύλης as autourgic is argued deliberately by Sarris.
22. The phrase ἔξω τῆς πύλης seems clearly a topographical reference point. Such landmarks are used in many cities and towns without a system of named streets. For instance, in San Jose, Costa Rica, directions are often given relative to a shuttered Coca-Cola bottling plant.
23. Sarris 2006, 63. Sarris arrives at this definition primarily by connecting the obligation to sow in *PSI*

labor and residence on Apion-owned land, does paint this picture: the *georgos* is to "remain permanently in attendance and abide upon the said *ktema* along with his loved ones and wife and cattle and all his gear, answerable to all (the responsibilities) that pertain to his person or to the condition of a registered agricultural labourer, and . . . is by no means to forsake the *ktema* or take himself off elsewhere."[24] Ruffini, however, notes that the term has a much wider semantic range than the one posited by Sarris: "This term is more neutrally and more frequently rendered simply as 'farmers.' Even this masks the range of social ranks the term can cover. Consider the Aphrodito *georgoi*: Gascou and MacCoull once noted the case of Daueid son of Biktor, attested as a *georgos* in the Aphrodito cadastre (520s CE), and also appearing in *P.Flor.* 3.280, from the previous decade, as a former *protokometes* or village-headman of Aphrodito. In other words, he was a member of the village elite, not a land-labourer. We see other *georgoi* in the Aphrodito papyri who are also monks, deacons, priests, *nomikoi*, even an *iatros*. The term clearly cannot be limited to peasant labor."[25]

It is possible that the usage of the word differed between Aphrodito and Oxyrhynchus, but among the Apion papyri as well, the status of the *georgoi* is more complicated than Sarris envisions it. In *P.Oxy.* 70.4794, published in the same year as Sarris' monograph, Aurelius Ieremias promises to provide surety for two *enapographoi georgoi*. In the document, Ieremias describes himself both as an *enapographos georgos* and as a former *meizon*, village headman. The *meizon* occupied a relatively high-status position, responsible for arbitration of disputes within a village and between villages, providing sureties for other villagers, and, in the sixth and seventh centuries, collecting taxes and helping to manage various aspects of the Apion estates.[26] In *P.Oxy.* 70.4794, Ieremias pledges πάντα μου τὰ ὑπάρχοντα καὶ ὑπάρξοντα ἰδικῶς καὶ γενικῶς ἐνεχύρου [λόγῳ καὶ ὑποθή]κ̣η̣ς δικαί[ῳ.[27] This phrase is formulaic, common in contracts and sureties after the fifth century, and pledges land in the case of default.[28] The

---

1.62, a surety guaranteeing the presence of an *enapographos georgos* on the Apion estate, with the lists of numbers of laborers required to sow *autourgia* in *P.Wash.Univ.* 2.102 and *P.Oxy.* 27.2478.

24. Sarris 2006, 61.

25. Ruffini 2009, 634. Elsewhere, Ruffini (2011, index, *s.v. georgos)* also lists numerous Aphrodito *georgoi* with various roles outside of peasant labor: e.g., Apollos 19 is a landholder, Apollos 38 a shepherd and a field guard.

26. Berkes, forthcoming.

27. This phrase is translated by the editors of *P.Oxy.* 70.4794 as "all my belongings present and future, in particular and in general, by way of security and by right of mortgage."

28. E.g., *CPR* 19.44; *P.Col.* 8.244; *P.Dubl.* 32, 33; *P.Michael* 34; *P.Oxy.* 1.125, 1.136, 1.138, 16.1895, 19.2238, 44.3204.

editor of *P.Oxy.* 16.1895 notes that ἰδικῶς καὶ γενικῶς means "'individually and generically,' i.e. the liability attached to the property as a whole and to all its items."[29] A ὑποθήκη is generally a mortgage on real property. This would confirm the note of the editor of *P.Oxy.* 70.4794 that "the wording . . . suggests that Ieremias may have owned land, and that he could possibly acquire more land in the future."[30] The evidence of a high-status Apion *enapographos georgos*, very likely to have owned his own land and maintained prospects of acquiring more, undermines Sarris' claims that the Apion *georgoi* were strictly wage laborers tied to the *ktema* that they were granted the privilege of leasing. Venticinque looks at the varied activities of a *georgos* named Pekusios who appears in *P.Oxy.* 16.1911 and 55.3804 and concludes that the Apion *georgoi* were more than strictly land laborers.[31] Pekusios leased land himself, worked imperial and *autourgia lands*, was a vinedresser and oil maker, and, in transactions with the state, represented associations of others engaged in these activities. Other *georgoi* appearing in the accounts, however, were not so varied in their undertakings. According to Venticinque, the estate viewed Pekusios as a man to be relied on and influential in his community. Both Venticinque's analysis of *georgoi* in the accounts and the differences in *P.Oxy.* 1.135 and *P.Oxy.* 70.4794 confirm, as is to be expected, that the reality of land tenure in Byzantine Oxyrhynchus was not monolithic. The differences not only between Oxyrhynchus and Aphrodito but also within Oxyrhynchus and the Apion dossier, as well as the many customary charges and payments in a single account, point up the variety of labor and land arrangements by which the land in Byzantine Egypt was exploited.

Of the four accounts surviving relatively intact, only two (*P.Oxy.* 16.1911 and 55.3804) show the *autourgia* playing a significant role in the expenditures portions. Those two documents—nearly identical in many sections—are actually accounts for the same portions of the estate, separated by some nine years, and cannot be counted as independent data points regarding the significance of the *autourgia* for the overall estate. Of the other two intact accounts, *P.Oxy.* 19.2243a makes no mention of the *autourgia*, and *P.Oxy.* 18.2195 mentions it only once, in line 133, in reference to hayseed bought for the "southern *autourgia*," not categorized separately from the other entries. The fragmentary accounts *PSI* 8.954 and *P.Oxy.* 18.2204, 16.1912, and 16.2019 make no mention of the *autourgia* ei-

29. *P.Oxy.* 16.1895.15 n. *P.Yale* 3.3 n. (p. 68) suggests the possibility that the phrase means "in cash and in kind."
30. *P.Oxy.* 70.4794.19–21 n.
31. Venticinque 2014.

ther, and the *autourgia* is mentioned explicitly only once in *P.Oxy.* 16.1913, again in relation to hayseed that had been purchased.[32] On such limited evidence, it seems overly confident to suggest that the entire purpose of the leased land that is well represented in the extant accounts was to support the needs of the comparatively little-documented *autourgia*.

Aspects of the two accounts that provide the most substantive evidence about the *autourgia*, *P.Oxy.* 16.1911 and 55.3804, undermine Sarris' fundamental claim that the *autourgia* appears only in the expenditures section of the account (which would indicate that the *ktemata* were meant to supply the *autourgia*). In both documents, the portions of the *autourgia* specifically named and delineated are each designated *edaphe*. Sarris notes, "It is primarily in relation to the *autourgia* that we find mention of the *edaphe*, implying that *edaphos* was the standard term for a subdivision of directly managed land."[33] Hickey disputes this, pointing out several instances in other papyri where leased land is classed as *edaphe*.[34] Even in *P.Oxy.* 55.3804, a number of named *edaphe* appear in the income portion; significantly, one, Pheltanbel, appears in both the income section (line 120) and the autourgic expenditures section (line 199).[35] The obvious conclusion to draw from this latter point is that *autourgia* land appears in both income and expenditures in the accounts. This contradicts Sarris' fundamental claim that ktematic land's exclusive role was supporting the *autourgia* and that "no document to date (as of 2010) reveals the *pronoêtai* to have handled productive arrears on the *autourgia*."[36] Sarris offers the possibility that these *edaphe* appearing in the expenditures portions "may have represented landholdings transferred to the *ktemata* of these settlements from their respective *autourgiai* in response to a shortage of land on the former."[37] But nothing about these entries favors this scenario over the straightforward explanation that both collections and expenditures could be made from those working the *autourgia*. If Sarris' explanation were the case, the designation of land as *autourgia* in *P.Oxy.* 16.1911 and 55.3804 would be curious, since it would mean that a supposedly outdated and inaccurate labeling of these portions of the estate persisted for at

32. Sarris contends that much of the account is actually referring to the *autourgia*. This point is discussed below.

33. Sarris 2006, 33.

34. Hickey 2012, 28 n. 44.

35. Hickey (2008, 97 n. 45) notes that this also undermines Sarris' claim that the income reflected in extant estate accounts is strictly ktematic.

36. Sarris 2011, 265–66.

37. Sarris 2006, 33.

least nine years after their actual status had changed to ktematic land. The two documents are the fullest evidence about the *autourgia* yet become exceptional under Sarris' model.

Labor and Leasing Arrangements

In keeping with the position that the leased ktematic lands surrounding the various *epoikia* associated with the estate were devoted to meeting the needs of the surplus-producing *autourgia*, Sarris argues that the inhabitants of the *epoikia* were, as part of their lease agreement, obliged to work on the *autourgia* for periods essentially determined by the lessor.[38] As evidence, Sarris points to *P.Wash.Univ.* 2.102, a list of the number of workers from certain *epoikia* required to sow the landlord's autourgic land.[39] The document clearly shows that workers came from the *epoikia* to sow the *autourgia*, but it does not show that the obligation was part of their leasing agreement. It is difficult to know what to make of the surprisingly small number of workers required from each *epoikion*, only one or two in each of the extant entries. If it were the general practice to oblige lessees from each *epoikion*, whose populations were in the neighborhood of a hundred people,[40] to sow the *autourgia*, one might expect more workers to be demanded from each *epoikion*.[41] Nevertheless, requiring extra workers during sowing can be explained without assuming that they were lessees obligated by their leases. Banaji argues convincingly that workers like those mentioned in *P.Wash.Univ.* 2.102 were laborers, casual or permanent, paid a wage in cash.[42] If fodder was the primary crop of the *autourgia*, as it is likely to have been,[43] labor would more likely have been casual, since the agricultural demands fluctuated seasonally. Much as "monks poured out of their desert monasteries into the Delta fields to work for a daily wage" during the harvest,[44] those living on the *epoikia* without a direct claim to the fruits of leased land and in need of some means of income (e.g., family members of lessees and landless workers living in

38. Sarris 2006, 63–66.
39. Sarris 2011, 267.
40. Ruffini 2008, 109, table 8.
41. The phrase τῆς γεουχικῆς αὐτουργίας might refer, however, not to *all* of the landlord's *autourgia* but to a portion understood by the parties involved.
42. Banaji 1999, 211–12. Banaji prefers to see them as permanent laborers but calls the two options "equally possible."
43. This point is discussed further below.
44. Bagnall 1993, 123 and n. 64.

epoikia) could be drawn on to work for a wage during periods of high need like the sowing or the harvest.[45]

This explanation also fits the orders and receipts for bread and wine rations that Sarris adduces in support of his contention that *epoikia* lessees were required to work the *autourgia* as part of their leases. *P.Oxy.* 16.2012 is a list of wine rations for people from several Apion-related *epoikia*. *P.Oxy.* 16.1952 and 72.4926–29 are orders and one receipt to the monastery of Musaeus for the supply of given amounts of bread to given numbers of people from several locations known from other Apion texts. Though no explicit indication of the purpose of these rations is given, the dates of the orders of bread coincide with the harvest, and the phrase λόγῳ τροφῆς in *P.Oxy.* 72.4927 argues against a charitable or festival context.[46] Even if it is granted that the rations were for agricultural workers, it is unclear whether the work was being performed in the locations mentioned or elsewhere on the estate.[47] Moreover, Sarris describes the locations mentioned in the documents as "various Apion *epoikia*,"[48] but this is not precisely accurate, since some of the locations named are *komai*, or villages, rather than *epoikia*. The population of a *kome* was larger than that of an *epoikion*, and unlike *epoikia*, a *kome* was not owned entirely by a single person or estate.[49] It is conceivable that along with people from the smaller *epoikia*, the populations of these villages, whether from the portions associated with the Apion estate or not, could be drawn on for casual labor in times of increased need.[50] But even if it is granted, further, that the work of those being given rations was to be performed away from the named locations and, instead, on the *autourgia*, it is still not clear that the workers are lessees rather than landless laborers seeking a wage. In short, these documents give no reason to think that the rations were associated with work obligations to the *autourgia* entailed in leases.

If Apion lessees were required to work on the *autourgia*, one would expect

45. The workers are called ἐργάται in *P.Wash.Univ.* 2.102. Banaji (1999, 198) notes that this "normal term for a casual worker . . . came to be used of permanent labourers as well" in late antiquity.

46. *P.Oxy.* 72, p. 173. This reasoning cannot be applied to *P.Oxy.* 16.2012, dated to September 30 / October 1, the time of sowing.

47. *P.Oxy.* 72, p. 173.

48. Sarris 2011, 267 n. 54.

49. Hickey 2012, 25 with refs. in n. 22.

50. The order for the most bread for the greatest number of people, *P.Oxy.* 72.4927, is for the village of Senokomis: 213 individuals are to be provided for there; *P.Oxy.* 16.1952, for the supply of an *epoikion* and *ktema*, is a close second at 200. Laura, a village, is supplied for 24 people; Meskanounios, Megalou Choriou, and Theagenous, all *epoikia*, are supplied for 50, 50, and 24, respectively.

to find the details of the arrangement—how many days were required, when, and where—in the documents relating to leases. Only four leases from the Apion estate survive, one of which is doubtfully attributed to the Apion dossier.[51] None of these leases mention an obligation to work any land aside from that being leased, nor do they discuss the *autourgia*. The paucity of leases from the Apion estate and from the fifth- and sixth-century Oxyrhynchite generally, compared to other document types and places in Egypt, may be the result of large estates in Oxyrhynchus shouldering out the smaller lessors and may indicate that leasing was on the wane as a model of land exploitation.[52] However, both the existence of ἀπαιτήσιμα (collection lists) and references from other documents to ἀπαιτήσιμα strongly suggest that leasing was still prevalent at the height of the Apion estate.[53] Incomplete sources may once again be to blame, but Rowlandson has offered the alternate explanation that leases might have been kept locally on the estates, rather than in the city of Oxyrhynchus proper, whose trash dumps are the provenance of most of the extant Apion documents.[54] She and Gonis have also argued that leasing did not disappear altogether. Instead, leases came to be documented in a different way than the lease agreements of earlier centuries. Gonis quotes Rowlandson: "As landlords grew more and more remote from their tenants and the terms under which their land was farmed perhaps became more standardised, the rent-roll replaced the lease as the most important record of their relationship."[55]

If Rowlandson's explanation is correct, then for leases drawn up according to the standard in the *apaitesima*, only the name, the location, and the amount collected would need to have been recorded in the *pronoetes* accounts; the rest of the details could be assumed as standard. Special situations diverging from the standard were recorded and noted in the accounts with special comments. This holds for both the receipts and expenditures sections. Hence, collections made according to the standardized agreements laid out in the *apaitesimon* were entered as names and amounts without further detail. If the lease was out of the ordinary, such as agreements involving the leasing of dovecotes or oil

51. *P.Flor.* 3.325; *P.Oxy.* 63.4390, 67.4615. *P.Oxy.* 16.1968 (= *SB* 26.16722) is only tentatively attributed to the Apion estate. See Gonis 2000 for a new edition and commentary.
52. See Gonis 2000, 95 n. 9, for relevant bibliography arguing this perspective.
53. Gonis 2000, 95. *P.Oxy.* 16.2037 is an ἀπαιτήσιμον. Rent rolls are referred to in several documents, e.g., *P.Oxy.* 55.3803, 16.1915, and 1.136 and *P.Bagnall* 33.10.
54. Rowlandson 1994, 498. Gonis (2000, 95 n. 8) calls the suggestion "ingenious, but difficult to prove."
55. Rowlandson 1994, 499, quoted in Gonis 2000, 95.

presses, ἀπότακτον χωρίων, or payment of a special tax, this was specified.[56] If there was to be a reduction of rent for customary reasons or damaged land, it was mentioned in the expenditures section, alongside charitable contributions and payments to artisans, skilled workers, and the purchase of provisions.[57] The consequence of this reading of the accounts is that those entries for which the accounts give the most detail ought to be regarded as exceptional, at least for the property administered by the *pronoetai*. Remissions on leased property appearing in the expenditures section, then, are all exceptional cases.

This leaves both the usual, least elaborate entries in the receipts section and the autourgic sections in the expenditures section of the *pronoetes* accounts as the source of evidence for the standard method of structuring the estates, against which other methods were measured. In some entries in the receipts portion of *P.Oxy.* 55.3804, collections for one *epoikion* are made from people originating from a different *epoikion*. There are Lukiu collections from people from Konkon, Apele, and Pekty; and there are Tarusebt collections from people from Apele and Lukiu.[58] To Sarris, these entries are evidence of "a deliberate policy of labour transfer between estate properties."[59] *P.Oxy.* 55.3804.196–202 records expenditures for *autourgia* related to Tarusebt, with certain entries showing that *autourgia* in Tarusebt was cultivated by people from Lukiu.[60] According to Sarris, therefore, the purpose of this transfer policy was to supply the *autourgia* with labor, and "it is likely to have been primarily the labour requirements of the *autourgia* that dictated the character and extent of labour transfers between the Apion-owned settlements."[61]

Evidence of people from one *epoikion* leasing land in another can, instead, explain why collections for one *epoikion* are made from people originating from a different *epoikion*. In *P.Oxy.* 55.3804.92, a collection is made from Isaac son of Melas from the *epoikion* Apele for ἰδίας γῆς—land he privately owned, not leased—in Lukiu. If Isaac could own land outside his *epoikion*, given the

56. E.g., *P.Oxy.* 55.3804 specifies a dovecote in line 31, date palms and a poll tax in line 46, an oil press in line 77, and sheep and a poll tax in line 93. On ἀπότακτον χωρίων, see Gascou 1985, 7–8; Hickey 2012, 53–58.

57. E.g., *P.Oxy.* 55.3804 mentions various concessions κατὰ τὸ ἔθος (according to custom) in lines 157–60, concession for unsuitable land in line 161, and concession for land destroyed by a broken dike in line 179. Hickey (2012, 53–58, especially 54) argues that the category of land called *apotakton chorion* is fixed-rent land owned by the imperial house and administered by the Apions.

58. *P.Oxy.* 55.3804.65, 84, 85, 86, 91; 116, 123.

59. Sarris 2006, 38.

60. *P.Oxy.* 55.3804.196–98.

61. Sarris 2006, 38.

varied economic statuses of *georgoi*, it is certainly conceivable that a relatively prosperous *georgos* might have leased land outside his own *epoikion*. If these people were not transferred from one *epoikion* to another, it is not necessary to connect them with the presence of people from different *epoikia* on Tarusebt's *autourgia*. Instead, they can be explained as the casual laborers suggested by the wine and bread rations and the list of laborers discussed above.[62] The picture of leasing and labor painted by the accounts supports that painted by the list of rations and laborers: some *georgoi* owned land, others leased land, some leased more land than others, and still others leased no land at all but worked for a wage when they could.

Expanding Estates

One of the consequences of the bipartite structure of the estates was, according to Sarris, an increase in the size of estates during the Byzantine period and, therefore, in the amount of land from which profits could be extracted. Larger estates were "conducive to . . . the more widespread introduction of direct forms of estate management, bipartite estates better suited to specialised production for the market."[63] Sarris' model therefore would be bolstered if expansion of the estates could be demonstrated. Jones attempted to estimate the size of the Apion estates by working back from the amount of the rate of *embole* taxation per *aroura* provided by *P.Cairo.* 67057 and from the total contribution from the *endoxos oikos* in the Oxyrhynchite and Cynopolite areas, presumably the Apion estate, known from *P.Oxy.* 1.127r. The figures at which he arrives indicate a massive estate, on the order of 112,000 arouras, or 120 square miles.[64] Hickey notes that these numbers are flawed in light of Gascou's model of fiscal shares, under which the *oikos* would have been responsible for collecting a share of the total tax burden, which entailed collections from neighboring holdings.[65] The total size of the Apion lands would therefore have been substantially smaller than the figure arrived at by Jones' calculation. Based on accounts of wine and land devoted to vines, Hickey estimates the amount of vine land on the Apion estate

62. *P.Oxy.* 16.2012, 16.1952, 72.4926–29; *P.Wash.Univ.* 2.102.
63. Sarris 2006, 198.
64. Jones 1964, 784.
65. Hickey (2012, 49) notes, "Even Sarris, Gascou's most vehement critic, acknowledges that the estate collected sums from settlements for which it was 'pagarchically responsible.'"

to have been between 245 *arouras* at the very low end and 1,172 *arouras* at the very high end, with somewhere in the range of 600 arouras being the likeliest figure.[66] In *P.Amh.* 2.79, a late second-century petition concerning misdeeds in the collection of grain by local magistrates, figures for the farmland and vineyard land making up one person's holdings are given, with vineyard accounting for about 2.8 percent of the total. On the assumption that the Apions devoted a similar percentage of their land to vineyards, the total amount of land making up the Apion estate was likely only about 21,000 *arouras,* less than 42,000 at most.[67] Hickey notes that given the Apions' higher social status than the parties involved in *P.Amh.* 2.79, we might expect a still greater proportion of land devoted to vineyards, which would mean even smaller estates.[68] Given the increased significance of mechanical irrigation in the sixth century as compared to the second century and the connection of mechanical irrigation with wine production, this supposition seems all the more secure.

The rather smaller estates that Hickey finds in the Oxyrhynchite correspond with the results of investigations into whether there is a discernible concentration of ownership from the Roman period through the end of the Byzantine period.[69] In an examination of fourth-century land lists from the Hermopolite, Bowman writes, "it is difficult to find any clear indication in the registers that the very wealthy were systematically absorbing the holdings of the less prosperous landowners to a more marked degree than earlier. . . . If the prime evidence for the development of the 'Byzantine large estate' can be found in the fourth century it will not come from the Hermopolite land-lists."[70] As Johnson and West argued before,[71] Rowlandson claims that modern scholars' assumption of increasingly concentrated landownership in the late Roman and Byzantine periods stems from the increasing frequency of the documentation associated with the estates, which does not necessarily correspond to an increase in the phenomenon itself.[72] There is, Rowlandson notes, no evidence to support the assumption.[73] Bagnall sums up the conclusion: "The phenomenon

66. Hickey 2001, 69; 2012, 22–27.
67. Hickey 2001, 71; 2012, 154.
68. Hickey 2001, 71.
69. When there is an essentially fixed amount of arable land, as was the case in Egypt (the floodwaters could only reach so much land, even with mechanical irrigation), concentration of ownership and expansion of estates are synonymous.
70. Bowman 1985, 155.
71. Johnson and West 1949, 65.
72. This skepticism falls into the second category of defective sources I discuss.
73. Rowlandson 1996, 281.

of concentration of ownership seems little changed from Roman times to the sixth century and tends to retreat into the future whenever confronted with evidence for any particular period."[74]

However, considering *P.Oxy.* 16.1915, a sixth-century account of land owned by the emperor but administered by the Apion estate, alongside *P.Oxy.* 27.2479, a petition from a *georgos* asking to be permitted to return to the farm he abandoned, Sarris sees evidence in the former that the Apions assumed ownership of land that had formerly been a possession of the imperial government.[75] The name of the *epoikion* Kineas appears in *P.Oxy.* 16.1915 and also turns up in *P.Oxy.* 27.2479. Sarris claims that *P.Oxy.* 27.2479 is the later of the two documents and that, by the time of its composition, an Apion should be identified as the owner, rather than the administrator, of the land mentioned in it. Taken together, the two documents show that "the land had been fully integrated into the Apion estates,"[76] and they therefore offer evidence of Apion expansion "at the expense of both private landowners and the imperial household."[77]

But the case is thin for the dating of *P.Oxy.* 27.2479 and for identifying an Apion as the owner, rather than administrator, of the *epoikion* mentioned in it. Sarris writes, "This is on the presumption that the δεσπότης invoked in *P.Oxy.* XXVII 2479, line 1 was the head of the Apion family rather than the emperor, in which case one might have expected a somewhat fuller and more elaborate descriptive address than τῷ ἐμῷ ἀγαθῷ εὐεργ(έτῃ) (καὶ) δεσπ(ότῃ). That this δεσπότης rather than a third party owned the estate in question is suggested by the fact that Pieous (the petitioner in *P.Oxy.* 27.2479) describes himself as *his* γεωργὸς ἐναπόγραφος (line 7). If the identification is correct, the document should be dated to after 560."[78] Three claims are made here: (1) that the addressee is not the emperor but an Apion, (2) that the land has come to be owned by the Apion estate, and (3) that the document was composed after *P.Oxy.* 16.1915. In the absence of other documents corroborating the first claim, one wonders how far to take such an argument. Even if it is granted, however, that the emperor is not the addressee, it does not necessarily follow that the imperial house is no longer the owner of the land, Sarris' second claim. The phrase γεω] ρ̣γὸς ἐναπό̣γραφος τυγχάνω τῆς ὑμ̣ετέρας π[α]νευκλ̣ε̣οῦς δεσποτείας in line 7,

74. Bagnall 1993, 160 n. 61.
75. See also Azzarello 2012, especially appendix 2, on *P.Oxy.* 16.1915, which includes new readings on lines 11–13.
76. Sarris 2006, 72.
77. Sarris 2006, 83.
78. Sarris 2006, 72 n. 8.

to which Sarris refers, could simply mean "an ἐναπόγραφος γεωργὸς under his charge," rather than denoting ownership of the land to which the γεωργός is registered. *P.Oxy.* 16.1867, a seventh-century letter to a village headman, contains the phrase τοῦ σὺν ὑμῖν δεσπότου ἡμῶν τοῦ ἀντιγεούχου ἐρχομέν[ο]υ̣, "upon the arrival of our master, the landlord's agent, who is with you." In this text, a person is explicitly called "our master" and, at the same time, explicitly said to be the agent of the landlord, not the landlord himself. This interpretation is all the more likely in *P.Oxy.* 27.2479 if ἐναπόγραφος signifies a fiscal relationship and if the administrator was responsible for various collections from the *georgos*. Moreover, other petitions use phrases similar to τῆς ὑμετέρας δεσποτείας simply as an honorific designation for people of particular importance or high status, not emphasizing ownership.[79]

In fact, nothing in *P.Oxy.* 27.2479 directly contradicts a continuation of the scenario in *P.Oxy.* 16.1915, in which the Apion estate managed both the private and public aspects of the administration of land owned by the imperial household.[80] Sarris offers three other documents (*P.Mert.* 2.96 and *PSI* 3.196 and 3.197) as evidence corroborating the acquisition of imperial land by the Apions, based on references in them to either Kineas or Pempo, two of the *epoikia* mentioned in *P.Oxy.* 16.1915.[81] However, none of these documents demonstrates clearly that the Apions owned the land, showing only that they were associated with it and treated as having some kind of authority over its administration. *PSI* 3.196, an order for payment, is explicitly said to come from ὁ θεῖος οἶκος, the imperial house, indicating that, at the time of its composition, it was under the arrangement seen in *P.Oxy.* 16.1915, the very opposite of the claim Sarris uses it to make.[82] Although the beneficiary of the payment is lost from *PSI* 3.197, the document is of the same layout as *PSI* 3.196 and is addressed to the same person. It can therefore be presumed, as the Italian editors do, that it was also from ὁ θεῖος οἶκος. Little in *P.Mert.* II 96, a letter asking for the return of a collector from Pempo to the city, suggests that Pempo is owned by the sender; the only fact it makes clear is that he has authority over the collector responsible for the

79. E.g., *SPP* 10.111; *P.Oxy.* 16.1866, 1867, 1939, 1940. See also Gascou 1985, 24, explaining the use of "servile" language in reference to landlords.

80. See Hickey 2012, 53–58, especially 54, arguing that *apotakton chorion* is land owned by the imperial house and administered by the Apions. This type of land is mentioned in *P.Oxy.* 16.1915 in connection with the *epoikion* of Pempo.

81. Sarris 2006, 83 n. 8.

82. Land described as θεῖος, ἅγιος, or ἔνδοξος is imperial, church owned, or privately owned, respectively.

epoikion, as one would expect of an administrator. Absent clear evidence to the contrary, any presumptions about the nature of the association between the Apions and the land around Pempo should align with the document in which that association is described explicitly, *P.Oxy.* 16.1915, where the association is strictly administrative. These documents show that the property lines are at the very least blurred, as Hickey describes them,[83] and that relying on them for evidence of expanding estates is hazardous.

Production on the Estates

Hickey highlights three areas as potential avenues for commercial agricultural engagement on the Apion estate: wheat, wine, and flax. In each of these areas, Hickey finds no evidence of attempts at or the possibility of commercialization. Wheat was grown for internal consumption and compulsory contributions, the estate did not produce enough wine to sell in great quantities, and flax production might have been significant on Apion land but was not exploited commercially by the estate itself. Sarris disputes Hickey's conclusion that evidence for commercialized agriculture on the estates is lacking.

Sarris objects that Hickey only considers what was grown on the ktematic lands, for which accounting records survive, and therefore ignores the vast majority of the estate's production, which would have come from the *autourgia*. The problem, which recurs in Sarris' model, is that there is no evidence for the scale of the *autourgia* or its production beyond fodder. Sarris' claims about both the nature and extent of wheat, wine, and fruit on the *autourgia* cannot be substantiated on the basis of the surviving papyri. The evidence he adduces for these crops relies wholly on the problematic identification of ἔξω τῆς πύλης with αὐτουργία ἔξω τῆς πύλης. With respect to flax, Sarris concedes that there is not much evidence but points to *P.Oxy.* 19.2243a, in which "a group of Apion estate workers is recorded to have purchased flax from the household."[84] The word to which Sarris refers is στιππῖον (for στυππεῖον) in line 26, which means not simply flax[85] but tow—processed flax used for, for example, rope, wicks, baskets, and mats.[86] Rather than flax, then, the *georgoi* gave the estate money

83. Hickey 2001, 45–46.
84. Sarris 2011, 270.
85. The word for flax is λίνον.
86. Pliny, *Nat. Hist.* 19.3.17: "*quod proximum cortici fuit, stuppa appellatur, deterioris lini, lucernarum fere*

for a small quantity of a processed flax product commonly used in many facets of rural and urban life. The presence and use of flax products like tow on the estate come as no surprise and do not necessarily indicate anything about the extent or location of flax cultivation on the estate.[87] It is difficult, therefore, to make the leap, based on this evidence, that the estate was involved in flax production. Sarris also adduces *P.Oxy.* 16.2033, an account with an entry concerning a quantity of tow. The papyrus has textual problems, making the line regarding tow difficult to interpret, but it seems to concern a purchase of tow by the estate,[88] indicating that flax was not produced on estate land in quantities sufficient to meet even its own needs.[89]

Hickey argues that flax may indeed have been a significant crop on certain portions of the Apion estate.[90] He relies chiefly on a set of four Apion documents in which the recipient of a loan agrees to pay interest in tow or in λινοκαλάμη, flax straw, another product of flax used much like tow. In two of those documents, *P.Oxy.* 8.1130 and 72.4918, the lender is an Alexandrian trader accustomed to doing business around Oxyrhynchus. In another, *P.Oxy.* 72.4922, a στιπποπραγματευτής, or tow dealer, extends a loan. On the model of the papyri concerning the Alexandrian trader, the editor of that document suggests supplementing a highly fragmentary line with language similar to the interest payment in linen. In *P.Laur.* 3.75, the recipient of a loan agrees to pay interest in λινοκαλάμη to his *pronoetes*. Given the relative ubiquity of tow in Egypt, it should not come as a surprise that someone might be in the business of selling it in and around Oxyrhynchus or that people should be in possession of it. Of finished textiles, Bagnall writes, "Good quality fabrics . . . served in antiquity also as a form of storing wealth, of keeping money in reserve. In that regard they were like items made of precious metals."[91] Dealers in linen and tow would have been uniquely suited to liquidating that sort of stored wealth. While the interest payments in the documents at hand were not in good-quality fabrics, the dealers would have been in a position to treat the base materials of textiles

luminibus aptior." See also *P.Mich.* 14.680 n. 3 and refs. The editor there says of στυππεῖον that "essentially it is the raw material of flax," quoting the Pliny reference, but it is properly the product of flax that has been scutched (beaten) and/or hackled (combed) to separate the linen from the tow. For a description of the process, see Pliny, *Nat. Hist.* 19.3.16–18.

87. Similarly, the provision of axles and cogwheels by the estate does not indicate that there was commercialized wood production on the estate.

88. Hickey (2012, 36) says that "it was certainly not a sale."

89. Sarris 2011, 270. On the difficulties of interpretation, see Hickey 2012, 36 and n. 104.

90. Hickey 2012, 34–35.

91. Bagnall 1993, 33.

as similarly liquid.[92] *P.Oxy.* 71.4831, dating from 429, provides evidence of interest payment made with another material unlikely to have been grown on the estate. The papyrus is an Oxyrhynchite loan to a person from a non-Apion *epoikion*, with interest to be paid in woad, a dye plant on which there was an apparent state monopoly.[93] There is evidence, then, that products obtained from outside the estate were used for interest payments. Flax products could well be put to similar use. But even if Hickey correctly posits that substantial amounts of flax were grown on the Apion estate, he argues that flax was produced on leased land, not on the *autourgia*.[94]

The great majority of the evidence about the *autourgia* points to fodder as its produce. A total of nine Oxyrhynchite papyri mention the *autourgia* and have been dated to the fourth century or later. *P.Oxy.* 16.1911, 16.1913, and 55.3804 are the *pronoetes* accounts discussed above. In *P.Oxy.* 16.1911 and 55.3804, where the *autourgia* is mentioned several times, either no crops are specified in connection with it, or it is mentioned in the context of a payment to field guards for watching over hay (55.3804.241) or for the price of hayseed for the *autourgia* (55.3804.244, 246). The sole mention of *autourgia* in *P.Oxy.* 16.1913 occurs in line 37, documenting a payment for the price of hayseed for the *autourgia*. *P.Oxy.* 14.1734, 18.2195, and 27.2480 are other Apion accounts in which the *autourgia* is connected explicitly and exclusively with fodder or hayseed.

Three documents mentioning the *autourgia* remain: *P.Wash.Univ.* 2.102 and *P.Oxy.* 16.1918 and 16.2032. *P.Wash.Univ.* 2.102, discussed above, is a brief list of the number of workers from certain *epoikia* who are obliged to sow the *autourgia* of the estate. What this document can tell us about the production of the *autourgia* is limited, but the evidence points toward fodder. Mazza has suggested emending the toponym identifying the place to which the workers must go to *Path*, short for *Path Tampenou*.[95] If this emendation is accepted, it may be significant that only fodder is attested from that place.[96] The last two documents, *P.Oxy.* 16.1918 and 16.2032, are part of the same papyrus account,

---

92. Considering the relatively small amounts involved in the interest, commodities of sufficient value might have been more readily at hand than billon.
93. *P.Oxy.* 71.4831 n. 13 and refs.
94. Hickey 2012, 35. Hickey uses the four documents mentioned above as evidence that flax was grown at all. He looks at the relatively higher proportion of cash receipts on portions of the estate associated with flax in different periods and concludes that cash rents on flax land were responsible for the differences. Hence, according to his argument, flax, if grown at all, was not grown on the *autourgia*.
95. Mazza 2001, 131.
96. Hickey 2012, 30 n. 63. The other attestations of Path Tampemou in the papyri are *P.Oxy.* 18.2195.132–33 and 55.3804.244–47.

16.1918 being a continuation and a classified summary of the figures in 16.2032. The document is a list of arrears (ἔχθεσις) in money, showing the amounts paid by various persons and groups against the remainder owed to the estate. Lines 68–90 are headed ἔχθ(εσις) τῆς αὐτουρ̣[γ]ί̣[ας]. It is not clear from the entries why money was owed to the estate. Most entries have a name, perhaps an occupation or an origin, and the amounts paid and owed. Sarris has suggested that the entries showing amounts owed by groups from *epoikia* appearing in other Apion documents "may represent sums owed by labourers with respect to payment for lodgings on the *autourgia*."[97] While such representation is possible, there is no evidence to support the suggestion. Moreover, given that the Apion estate collected taxes for land it did not own, it is not clear that the Apions must be assumed to have owned an *epoikion* mentioned in an Apion account.[98] These entries can tell us little about what was being grown on the *autourgia*.

In two of the entries in *P.Oxy.* 16.2032, however, a commodity is mentioned in connection with the arrears. Line 72 is damaged but preserves a name, the word σίτου, and the amount of the arrears. Line 75 has a name, occupation, and origin and notes that the arrears are for the price of *arakos*, a type of legume eaten by people but also frequently used as fodder.[99] Still, the exact situation that brought these people to owe money to the estate is not clear. Hickey has examined entries outside the *autourgia* section of the account, for arrears owed by a Pamouthis for the price of wine, and offered two possible readings: either the money had been advanced to Pamouthis to purchase wine, or wine had been advanced, and proceeds from its sale were owed the estate.[100] Both types of activity are attested in other documents, but the former is rather more likely, since Pamouthis would be assuming a much larger liability than other such sales on credit.[101] The way Pamouthis acquired the wine may clarify the two *autourgia* arrears entries for which types of produce are mentioned. Both people in those entries are ναῦται.[102] Like Pamouthis, the two might have been advanced money for the transport costs associated with the acquisition of wheat and *arakos*. Specialized purchasers of

97. Sarris 2006, 42.
98. Ruffini (2010, 634) notes, "We must be aware of the Apionic gravitational pull, and resist adding to Apionic property every toponym appearing in an Apionic text."
99. On *arakos*, see Bagnall 1993, 26 and nn. 68–69. See also Hickey 2012, 31.
100. Hickey 2012, 142–43.
101. Hickey 2012, 143–44.
102. In line 72, the occupation is restored by the editors to ν[αύτ(η.

fodder, χορτοπαραλῆμπται, are attested as having traveled large distances to acquire fodder, and if the *autourgia* did not produce wheat, it is conceivable that the taxes in kind owed on it might have been acquired from without.[103] Indeed, if the *autourgia* did not grow wheat of its own but was still liable for obligations valued in that commodity, the wheat would need to be supplied from elsewhere. As Sarris emphasizes, the *autourgia* appears predominantly in the expenditures portions of accounts rather than in the receipts, a fact that can be explained if the *autourgia* did not produce wheat of its own. If, as Hickey notes, the land in the accounts did not produce much surplus in wheat beyond its owners' own fiscal obligations,[104] autourgic need would have to be met from outside of the estate. The possibility that the fiscal dues on autourgic land were paid through *adaeratio*—that is, paid in cash of an equivalent value to the grain owed—would similarly entail the estate drawing on other parts of its enterprise to provide the necessary cash.[105]

Rethinking the Purpose of the Autourgia

Sarris argues rightly, then, that the leased lands did support the autourgic land, but in the more limited sense of covering its tax liability. The evidence points strongly to fodder, rather than a variety of cash crops, as the primary product of the *autourgia*. That the estate bought seed for fodder makes it difficult to see how it could have been the main source of Apion wealth. If the evidence in the papyri supports a more circumscribed role for the *autourgia* than Sarris contends, is it possible to determine what that role might have been? Hickey suggests that the association with fodder might indicate a centralized transportation system used on the estates, wherein feed for the transport animals was grown on the *autourgia* and used throughout the leased lands associated with the estate.[106] Given the significance of artificial irrigation on these estates[107] and the integral role that beasts of burden played in the operation of the irrigation

103. Hickey 2012, 30–31.
104. Hickey 2012, 29.
105. It is unlikely that proceeds from the sale of excess fodder was devoted to the fiscal obligations, since the purchase of fodder seed suggests that the estate was unable to meet its own needs.
106. Hickey 2008, 97 n. 45.
107. Hickey (2007, 293–94) notes that "the aristocrats invested heavily in the *saqiya* [*mechane*], which might be considered the hallmark of their estates."

machines, as well as the centralized system of rent and tax collection,[108] a centralized system of fodder production should not be surprising.

P.Oxy. 16.1913 (mid-sixth century) is the expenditures portion of an Apion account similar to *pronoetes* accounts such as *P.Oxy.* 16.1911 and 55.3804. Its first five lines indicate the centralized use of animals for irrigation, which would argue in favor of some centralized system of obtaining fodder for their feed. The entry concerns a remission of rent for a certain group of farmers who were granted a plot of artificially irrigated land designated for fodder.

> συνẹχωρήθ(η) τοῖς γεωρ(γοῖς) ἔξω τῆς πύλης ὑπὲρ τῆς μηχ(ανῆς) σπειρομ(ένης) ποτὲ π(αρὰ) Πέτρου καὶ κληρονόμ(ων) ἄπα Νακίου δ(ιὰ) τὸ τὰς ἀρούρ(ας) τῆς αὐτ(ῆς) μηχ(ανῆς) δοθ(ῆναι) τοῖς εἰρημ(ένοις) γεωργοῖς λόγ(ῳ) ἐνχόρτου, ὑπὲρ οὗ τὴν ἄρδ̣ẹ(υσιν) ποιήσ(ονται) εἰς τὰ πωμάρ(ια) καὶ εἰς τὰ χωρ(ία) ἐκ τῶν ἰδίων αὐτῶν κτηνῶν ἀντὶ τῶν γεουχικ(ῶν) βοειδ(ίων) τοῦ ἐνδόξ(ου) οἴκ(ου) καὶ ἐπὶ τῆς γ ἰνδ(ικτίονος) σίτου κ(αγκέλλῳ) (ἀρτάβαι) κα ∠.

> [Conceded to the cultivators Outside the Gate for the plot of irrigated land once sown by Peter and the heirs of *apa* Nakios because of the fact that the *arouras* of the same plot of irrigated land were transferred to the aforementioned farmers on account of its being land under grass, because of which they will provide irrigation to the orchards and to the vineyards from their own livestock in place of the landlord's oxen from the illustrious house, in the third indiction 21½ *art. canc.* wheat.]

Sarris understands these lines to indicate that "a group of agricultural workers were obliged to work a section of the *autourgia*, irrigating it themselves with the aid of their own oxen, in return for payment in kind and access to a piece of land."[109] Setting aside whether the land in question ought to be identified as *autourgia*,[110] this explanation does not accord with the meaning of similar entries in other accounts. Information about land leased out by the estate only appears in the expenditures section of estate accounts in special circumstances, such as when the land had been damaged or when a customary arrangement

108. The agents collecting taxes and rents in kind from the numerous geographically dispersed lease properties would have required some means of transport to a central location.

109. Sarris 2006, 39.

110. This is an instance where Sarris has identified ἔξω τῆς πύλης with αὐτουργία ἔξω τῆς πύλης.

was in place.[111] When such concessions were made due to some sort of extenuating circumstance, rather than custom, a fairly standard formula is followed: the entry identifies the *georgos* or *georgoi* by name or origin, names the land in question, and then provides the reason, date, and amount for the concession, as in *P.Oxy.* 55.3804.188–90.

> συνεχωρήθ(η) Ἰωάννῃ καὶ Ἡρακλείῳ ἀπὸ κτήμα(τος) Λουκίου ὑπὲρ τῆς ἀφανισθ(είσης) αὐτῶν γῆς τοῦ δικαίου
>
> τῆς μηχ(ανῆς) Ναυατὲ διαφερούσ(ης) τῷ αὐτῷ κτήμα(τι) Λουκίου ὑπὸ τῆς διακοπῆς τῶν χωμάτ(ων)
>
> ἐπὶ τῆς ιγ ἰνδ(ικτίωνος) ὑπὲρ (ἀρουρῶν) γ νο(μίσματα) β δ´ καὶ ἐπὶ τῆς ιδ ἰνδ(ικτίωνος) νο(μίσματα) β δ´.
>
> [Conceded to John and Heraclius from the holding of Lukiu, on account of their land in the *dikaion* of the irrigated land of Nauate in the same holding of Lukiu, which was destroyed, carried off by a breach in the dikes, in the thirteenth indiction, regarding 3 *arouras*, 2¼ *solidi*, and for the fourteenth indiction, 2¼ *solidi*.]

In cases where the occupant of the land has changed or possession has been complicated in some way, the reason for the complication is briefly explained, as in *P.Oxy.* 55.3804.169–70.

> συνεχωρήθ(η) τοῖς γεωρ(γοῖς) μηχ(ανῆς) τοῦ νέου λάκκου ἐν ἐποικ(ίῳ) Κοτυλεείου σπειρομέ(νης) ποτὲ
>
> π(αρὰ) Σμαράγδου νοταρ(ίου), νυνὶ δὲ δ(ιὰ) Παύλου Κουειέχος ἀκολούθ(ως) τύπῳ δοθ(έντι) αὐτῷ . . .
>
> [Conceded to the cultivators of the irrigated land of the new cistern in the *epoikion* of Kotyleeiu, once sown by Smaragdos, *notarius*, but now through Paul son of Kueiechos in conformity with the authority granted him . . .]

111. This fact alone should cast some suspicion on Sarris' interpretation, since he describes his model's usual case, not an exception.

Lines 1–5 of *P.Oxy.* 16.1913, concerning the use of cattle, follow this same pattern, but the custody of the land has changed in a way still more complex than in *P.Oxy.* 55.3804.169–70. It appears that a plot of land had been leased to and sown by one group—Peter and the heirs of *apa* Nikios—and subsequently allowed to go to grass. Because it had gone to grass, the lease of the land was transferred to another group, the "cultivators Outside the Gate." Part of the lease agreement required the group to supply water to the adjacent gardens and vineyards, using their own animals for the irrigation machinery. Such specifics about the land and lease agreements do not normally appear in the terse expenditure accounts unless there is something exceptional about the concession in them. For instance, in *P.Oxy.* 55.3804, concessions are given when part of the land was washed away because of a broken dike, a customary special arrangement was observed, or unsuitable areas of soil were present. In *P.Oxy.* 55.3804 (lines 163 and 175), portions of leased land described as *enchortos*, usually translated "overgrown with grass" or "under grass," were also treated as unsuitable for producing crops and therefore deserving of a remission of rent.[112] The plot of land in *P.Oxy.* 16.1913.1–5 is *enchortos* and therefore "damaged," but it is also classed as *mechane*, the standard term in the Byzantine papyri for land equipped with irrigation machinery.[113] Therefore, even if this land were no longer productive itself, it would have retained some value, because it could still supply water to adjacent vineyards, gardens, and fields.

Lines 1–5 of *P.Oxy.* 16.1913 appear in the expenditures section of an account because they designate an exceptional case, and the two specifics of the lease agreement explain precisely how it is exceptional: the leased land was defective but had irrigation machinery, and the cultivators were using their own oxen rather than the estate's for the irrigation of adjacent land. That the use of their own animals is specified as an exceptional circumstance indicates that lessees normally used the estate's animals for irrigation. A non-Apion lease from Oxyrhynchus dated to 411, *P.Oxy.* 55.3803, in which a plot of land with an irrigation machine is being leased, supports this conclusion. The terms of that agreement grant the lessee the use of one yoke of oxen (i.e., two animals). The irrigation machine referred to is the *saqiya*, which usually required two teams of two

112. That the Apions did not collect taxes for land under grass could also explain why the *autourgia*, associated with fodder, is mostly absent from the collections portions of the accounts.

113. Perhaps control of land gone to grass was assumed by the estates in order to assure control over fodder. See Rowlandson 1996, 23, for the agricultural importance of maintaining a fodder supply. See *P.Oxy.* 16.1831, 16.1913, and 55.3803 and commentary, for further examples of *mechanai* as land.

oxen, used in shifts.[114] Line 18 of the document further stipulates that the lessee is leasing half of the irrigation machine and therefore only one yoke of oxen.[115]

The other Apion lease for which the terms are extant, *P.Oxy.* 63.4390, does not mention the leasing of oxen, nor do the other published Oxyrhynchite leases of irrigation machines with land (*P.Mich.* 11.611; *P.Flor.* 3.325; *PSI* 1.77; *P.Berl.Zill.* 7; *P.Oxy.* 58.3955). Perhaps the irregular nature of the lease in *P.Oxy.* 55.3803—only half of the irrigation machine was being leased—called for the specification of how many oxen were included in the lease. The adjective ὁλόκληρος usually modifies the noun μηχανή in each of these leases, which would indicate that the entire machine, including both yokes of oxen, was being leased.[116] Essentially, the cultivators in *P.Oxy.* 16.1913.1–5 were leasing unproductive land from which they could still derive some income owing to its irrigation machinery. The situation is on the model of the irrigation agreements found in leases of the Roman period. From the advent of large-scale mechanical irrigation, arrangements were commonly undertaken to share water raised by irrigation machinery, since the costly machines often lifted more water than could be used on the piece of land to which they belonged and since the plots of land owned or leased by an individual were not always contiguous. For example, *P.Ross.Georg.* 2.19, of 141 CE, is a lease of partially damaged orchard and vine land under mechanical irrigation. As part of the lease agreement in that document, the lessee was permitted to make arrangements to sell the lifted water to neighbors and thereby recoup some of the lost production. Because lessees in such a case would derive less income than from productive land and had to take on the cost of owning and maintaining draft animals instead of using the estate's, they were deserving of a partial remission of the usual rent on the property.[117]

Early in the use of animal-driven irrigation machines, during the first and second centuries CE, it is clear that even without centralized control of farm-

114. On mechanical irrigation in Egypt, especially the *saqiya* and its identification in the papyri, see Oleson 1984; Bonneau 1993.

115. See *P.Oxy.* 55.3803.7 n.

116. Preisigke's *Wörterbuch* glosses as a parallel usage of the word *P.Cair.Masp.* 2.67170, τὸ ὑπάρχọν τῷ ὑφ' [ὑ]μ[ᾶς] ẹ[ὐα]γεῖ μογ(αστηρίῳ) ὁλόκληρọν πωμάριο\ν / . . . σὺν λ̣[ά]ḳκῳ ὁλοḳλ̣[ήρῳ], which Preisigke translates as "der Obstgarten gehört dem Kloster ungeteilt, ebenso zugehörige Brunnen." *P.Mich.* 11.611 is the lone instance where ὁλόκληρος is absent. In that text, μηχανήν follows a damaged portion of the papyrus, for which the editor suggests supplementing ἀ<ντ>λ[ητι]κήν. In *P.Oxy.* 16.1968, a fragmentary lease that includes land and an irrigator, the adjective modifies the *arouras* rather than the machine: ὁλοκλήρους ἓξ ἀρούρας οὔσας ἐν μηχανῇ καλουμέ(νῃ) τοῦ Μοναστηρίου.

117. On the substantial costs of maintaining oxen, see Rowlandson 1996, 23.

land, economies of scale were sought in the use of oxen. Rather than owning its own oxen to be used only for certain seasonal purposes, the estate of Epimachus leased them.[118] A centralized infrastructure for fodder production on the Apion estate might indicate that the earlier system was subsumed into the new situation of large-scale control of arable land by a single *oikos*.[119] Rather than having each lessee maintain his own set of oxen, a highly expensive arrangement that would have limited the pool of lessees to those with enough capital to own their own oxen, the estate itself maintained the oxen and the feed that was necessary for them. Leasing animals to neighboring smallholders in addition to tenants would have provided another revenue stream for the estate. Infrastructure for feeding and maintaining animals would have facilitated the centralized collection from smaller landholders and lessees of both rents and taxes, which often came not in cash but in kind and would therefore have required a means of transportation for the large volumes of grain.

P.Oxy. 16.1913 indicates that use of the estate's oxen was not the only option. Other documents show clearly that there were *enapographoi georgoi* who owned their own cattle.[120] The Apion documents provide evidence that there were some *enapographoi georgoi* who owned land *and* cattle, some who owned land *or* cattle, and some who owned neither land nor cattle. The Apion evidence, like the Aphrodito evidence, points to *georgoi* of various social and economic statuses. Likewise, the Apion evidence shows that the estate had mechanisms in place to accommodate varied arrangements with cultivators of such varying status.

Conclusion

This chapter began with a description of the broad categories of defects that might be present in the papyrological record of the Apion estate near Oxyrhynchus, Sarris' model being the latest and fullest exemplar highlighting the weaknesses arising from severely incomplete documentation. Sarris' explanation of the discrepancy between the wealth the Apions attained and the avenues of

118. Kehoe 1992, 62–63.

119. Control of land is not necessarily the same as owning it. In addition to fiscal control over the taxes to be collected from private landholders, there is leverage from those dependent on the estate for water access.

120. E.g., *P.Oxy.* 1.135, 27.2479, 70.4790–91.

wealth apparent in the papyrological documentation of their Oxyrhynchus holdings posits that the record overrepresents the ktematic lands. Sarris concludes that the *autourgia* made up a significant portion of the estates, produced a wide variety of cash crops, and was worked by cultivators obliged by their leasing agreements for ktematic land to till the autourgic land. His view is that the estate's "footprint" expanded from the fifth through seventh centuries as a result of its bipartite structure. This chapter argues, instead, that the *autourgia* was primarily devoted to producing fodder for estate-owned animals used by lessees and employees and that its produce was not the source of Apion wealth. I have further argued that the *autourgia* was sown and harvested mostly by casual wage laborers drawn from the *epoikia* and *komai* associated with the estate, likely from the nonleasing population living in those places. The *georgoi* who did lease and live in the Apion-associated *epoikia* and *komai* were not of homogenous social and economic status, and the types of arrangements possible with the estate were similarly varied. Without the bipartite structure, expanding landownership by estates should not be seen as necessary, and the evidence does not support Sarris' proposition.

CHAPTER 3

Benefits from Lower-Level Collections

If documents recording the vast and varied production of the *autourgia* have not been lost and if the papyrological record of the Apion estate does broadly represent how their estate in Oxyrhynchus functioned, the source of Apion wealth remains to be found. The relationship of the Apion estate with the imperial government is a promising area in which to look for that source. Since the social and political fortune of the Apion family, especially under Apion II, was tied to its relationship with the imperial family, it is reasonable to investigate the extent to which their economic success was also tied to that relationship. Gascou's model of fiscal shares has demonstrated the economic entanglement resulting from the Apions' collection of taxes on the government's behalf. It can be safely assumed that absent either reward or compulsion, the Apions and other estate owners would not have undertaken the difficult, time-consuming, and sometimes risky endeavor of collecting taxes. The nature of the evidence that has survived does not offer many insights into whether or how the imperial government might have compelled large landholders to do the state's bidding. The papyrus accounts, letters, and contracts do, however, offer a view into how collecting taxes benefited the Apion estate.

This chapter and chapter 4 examine the benefits that accrued to the estate from collecting taxes. These benefits could be intrinsic (estates could extract transaction fees from those whose taxes they collected and those who collected the taxes), extrinsic (imperial government could remunerate and promote those who ensured regular and efficient collection of taxes), or both. More specifically, the benefits intrinsic to the Apion system of collection are those that come to the estate from within its own collection apparatus, drawn from its collectors and those under its collection umbrella—that is, from the bottom up to the estate. They are distinct from the extrinsic benefits that come from their arrangement with the state to collect on its behalf—that is, from the top down to the estate. The combination of these two types of benefits amounts to the estate's total profit. I discuss the evidence for intrinsic benefits in this chapter and the evidence for extrinsic benefits in chapter 4.

The *pronoetes* accounts best document the lower-level functioning of the estates, and the structure of these accounts and their relation to the few extant accounts documenting the higher management level are the first places to look for intrinsic benefits of tax collection. The *pronoetes* accounts' conversion of grain from one type of *artaba* (a unit of dry measure) to another offers an avenue by which the *pronoetai* and, by extension, the estates made money. *Adaeratio,* the practice of meeting grain taxes by paying an equivalent sum in money, also allowed the estates to transmute their wheat produce into cash without directly engaging in market activities. This chapter describes how *pronoetai* were able to extract both money and produce from those beneath them and how the estates, in turn, extracted further cash and produce from the *pronoetai.* A fourth-century archive illustrates precisely how such a system developed and functioned in the century before the Apions first appear. By comparing upper- and lower-level Apion accounts, we can estimate the number of *prostasiai* on the Apion estate in the Oxyrhynchite and, thereby, the scale of the benefits intrinsic to the Apion system of tax collection. In the final analysis, that the number of Apion *prostasiai* greatly increased over the sixth century indicates that the area over which the Apions had collection responsibilities expanded, explaining the increase in collections apparent in the higher-level accounts.[1]

The Accounts of the Pronoetai

The papyri in the Apion dossier that most thoroughly document tax collection on the estate are the accounts of the *pronoetai.*[2] How these information-rich documents functioned on their own or in the larger context of the estates is not,

1. This expanded collection responsibility should not be equated to expanded ownership or concentration of ownership.
2. *P.Oxy.* 55.3804 and 16.1911 are the fullest and clearest in their organization. Other such accounts are *P.Oxy.* 18.2195, 19.2243a., and 16.1912–14. See Mazza 2001, 192, appendix 8, for an exhaustive table of the *pronoetes* accounts.

however, immediately apparent. With the exception of the extremely thorough commentary and presentation of *P.Oxy.* 55.3804, their editions are not always as full as one might hope.[3] This section of this chapter aims to explicate how these accounts related to actual practices on the estates and to clarify certain aspects of the terminology used in them.

The Apion estate was divided into a number of administrative units called *prostasiai*, comprising a handful of *epoikia* (hamlets) or parts of *komai* (villages). A *pronoetes* oversaw the collection of gold and grain for each *prostasia*.[4] Collections were made according to a list called an *apaitesimon*, generated at a higher level of administration.[5] The method of accounting used in the *pronoetes* accounts avoided altering the receipts side even when collections were not made according to the *apaitesima*. Instead, *pronoetai* dealt with changes in inflow by counting them as remissions on the expenditures side. Money not actually collected as demanded on the *apaitesimon* was still entered as collected on the receipts side and was then also entered as a remission on the expenses side. In other words, failure to collect was treated as an expense canceling out a notional, or target, receipt.[6] The practice results in such stability in the target collections that the total receipts in *P.Oxy.* 16.1911 and 55.3804, separated by nine years, are identical down to the last *choinix* and *denarius*.[7] As will be further discussed below, the solvency of the estates depended on the careful construction of the *apaitesima*. The way of operating evinced in the accounts, which "seems to us a peculiar method," can perhaps be attributed to the fact that the receipts side of the accounts would have been largely similar to the "fossilized" *apaitesima* governing them.[8]

The receipt portions of these texts (i.e., the *lemmata*) were discussed in the previous chapter, primarily in relation to rents for *ktemata* collected from residents of *epoikia* associated with the Apion estate. A payment collected by a *pronoetes* for ἰδίας γῆς, private land, indicates that he was responsible for collecting something that was not rent and that was payable by the owner of the

3. Those accounts appearing in *P.Oxy.* 16 are without translation and are often without commentary or line breaks. Those with commentaries, such as 1911, often focus on mistakes of arithmetic committed by the scribe.
4. See Hickey 2012, 25–27, for more on the division and classification of estate land.
5. *P.Oxy.* 16.2037 is an *apaitesimon*.
6. Describing the gross receipts, exclusive of remissions, as "target receipts" follows Hickey.
7. The *denarii* are converted to different amounts of solidi, however, likely due to changes in the rates of conversion of billon to gold coin over the nine years. See *P.Oxy.* 55.3804.272 n.
8. Hardy 1931, 100 ("peculiar"); Hickey 2008, 90 n. 12 ("fossilized"). The *apaitesima* were carefully constructed and rarely changed.

land, presumably a tax.[9] The Apion estate made collections of grain in villages in which they were unlikely to have owned property, and a handful of entries in the accounts explicitly describe the collections as being for taxes of one type or another.[10] The accounts, then, reflect not only rent collected on pieces of land but also taxes collected in both grain and money. The formulaic language of leases surviving from Apion and non-Apion Oxyrhynchite estates show that the lessor, not the lessee, was usually responsible for paying the taxes on the land.[11] Thus a collection appearing in the *lemmata* of a *pronoetes* account could reflect rent or taxes alone or both rent and taxes together.

Into which of these categories a particular *lemma* falls is undifferentiated in the *pronoetes* accounts.[12] This disregard for category distinctions can be explained under Gascou's model of taxation through fiscal shares, wherein the Apion estate, along with other large landholders, were responsible for paying and therefore collecting a given share of the total tax burden for the *nome*.[13] Whether the Apions would collect only rent, only taxes, or both rent and taxes from someone was determined by the tenure of the land, but the aggregate amount that they paid to the state was not. The *pronoetai* were told who was supposed to pay and how much. As long as the *apaitesima* (collection lists) were constructed in such a way that, in the aggregate, the tax revenue plus the rent revenue would cover expenses in grain and the estate's share of taxes, it was not necessary to separate rents from taxes upon collection. For the purposes of the *pronoetes* accounts, then, it was immaterial whether the collection was for rent or tax. One of Gascou's major contributions was pointing out that it is difficult to distinguish between taxes and rents in the accounts precisely because the two facets of economic activity were so inextricably linked for the estate.[14] Because the *pronoetai* did not treat the collections of taxes and rents as fundamentally different activities, the more relevant distinction is between collections in kind and collections in money. That distinction is emphasized in the

9. *P.Oxy.* 55.3804.92 = 16.1911.22. For other collections on ἰδίας γῆς, see *P.Oxy.* 16.1912.87; 16.2032.10, 29, and 31. On these collections, see Hardy 1931, 53. On identifying such a collection as a tax, see Hickey 2008, 49 n. 61.
10. Hickey 2008, 89 and *passim*; Hardy 1931, 52 with refs. in nn. 1 and 2.
11. *P.Flor.* 3.325 and *P.Oxy.* 63.4390 (both Apion) and *P.Oxy.* 6.913 (not Apion, but from fifth-century Oxyrhynchus) stipulate that the lessor is to pay the taxes. The other Apion leases do not contradict these documents but either do not survive intact or refer to usual practices from the ἀπαιτήσιμα. The cost of the taxes could, however, be priced into the lease, making the lessee the ultimate bearer of the burden.
12. The instances cited in n. 10 are exceptions.
13. Gascou 1985, 48 and *passim*.
14. Gascou 1985, especially 12–13.

accounts themselves, both in the notation of individual receipts and expenditures and in the management of surpluses.

While sorting taxes from rents in the *lemmata* is difficult, it is clear that taxes paid in grain and taxes paid in money were handled differently by the *pronoetai*.[15] *P.Oxy.* 1.126, a non-Apion document from 572, is a transfer of taxation from a father to his daughter for land given to her as dowry. The document shows the broad division of taxes for which a landowner was liable in sixth-century Oxyrhynchus, and unlike the accounts of the *pronoetai*, it treats taxes in isolation. Stephanous, the daughter, agrees to pay 63 artabas for *embole*—the grain taxes for the provisioning of Constantinople and Alexandria—and two types of money taxes: 22 *keratia* on the public standard for the *kanonika* to the *ethnikos* and 24 *keratia* (= 1 *solidus*) on the public standard for *arkarika* to the "*arkarios* or *embolator*."[16] The Apions and the landowners from whom they collected would have been similarly liable for these money taxes on the land, but payments for taxes in money do not appear in the expenditures section of the *pronoetes* accounts.[17] At the end of both *P.Oxy.* 16.1911 and 55.3804 (the best-preserved *pronoetes* accounts), the scribe writes that he has passed along the surplus money to the estate *trapezites* (banker) in installments over the course of the year, indicating that there was a larger pool of money collected from the estate's several *pronoetai* and that a higher level of administration drew on that pool to pay taxes in money.[18]

In contrast, the grain for *embole* was handed over by the *pronoetes* to an official called the *embolator* or directly to the public boatmen for transport and appears in the accounts as a single item of expenditure.[19] The *pronoetes* accounts balance in grain, either because receipts match expenditures (*P.Oxy.* 55.3804) or because the small surplus has been sold to the *embolator* (*P.Oxy.* 16.1911), the same official to whom Stephanous in *P.Oxy.* 1.126 was to pay the

15. Hardy 1931, 51–52; Hickey 2012, 50 n. 63.

16. *P.Oxy.* 1.126.10–16. On the *kanonika* and *arkarika*, respectively, see Johnson and West 1949, 309–10, 302–3. On the *embolator*, see Hickey 2008, 110. The system of different standards for the *solidus* used in the Apion dossier is extremely complex and not wholly understood. The commentary on lines 7–8 of *P.Oxy.* 55.3805 gives a detailed summary of the issues and attempts to shed light on a number of the problems. See also West and Johnson 1944, 140–57.

17. The exception is the small fee (about 1 *solidus* per 150 *kankellos* artabas) paid to the boatmen for the transportation of *embole* grain.

18. See the discussion below of *P.Oxy.* 18.2196.v and 16.1918, accounts from these higher levels. How the taxes were likely paid is discussed in chapters 4 and 5 as a tax-farming arrangement.

19. The following expenditure appears in *P.Oxy.* 55.3804.149: τοῖς κληρ(ονόμοις) Μηνᾶ ναύτου ἀπὸ Κόμα ὑπὲρ ἐμβολ(ῆς) ἀπὸ γενήμα(τος) ιδ ἰνδ(ικτίωνος) σίτ(ου) κ(αγκέλλῳ) (ἀρτάβαι) ρϙβ ⊠ χο(ίνικες) ζ.

arkarika. The proceeds from the sale were handed over by the *pronoetes* to the estate *trapezites*, and the grain was handed over by the *embolator* to the boatmen (*P.Oxy.* 16.1914).[20] At the end of each of these accounts where the end survives, the scribe writes πλήρης ὁ σῖτος, "the wheat is balanced."[21] The procedure, then, was as follows: grain remaining after payments to charity and other local expenses went first to the *embole*, so that as much of that obligation as possible could be met in kind rather than through *adaeratio*, the practice of paying amounts owed in kind with its equivalent value in money;[22] any further surplus in grain that remained beyond the payment for the *embole* would be sold to the *embolator*. In reality, then, all of the grain actually collected by the *pronoetai*, less charity and local expenses, went to the boatmen bound for Alexandria, either directly or through the *embolator*, who gave a cash refund on any amount of grain beyond that required for the *embole*.[23]

That all of the grain collected by the *pronoetai* went to the boatmen, either for the *embole* or in exchange for cash, can explain the absence of *analomata sitou*, grain expenditures, in the higher-level accounts. One such account, *P.Oxy.* 18.2195.v, records the sum of the *lemmata* in grain and both *lemmata* and *analomata* in cash from all of the Apions' Oxyrhynchite holdings.[24] Hickey has noted that "it is not readily apparent why the taxes were later entered for the *argyrika* [money taxes] but not for the grain."[25] He explains that grain expenditures may be absent at the higher levels of accounting because surplus grain was reserved for the *embole*.[26] But the grain surpluses after the *embole* payment in *P.Oxy.* 16.1911 and 16.1914 militate against this suggestion, and the grain account in *P.Oxy.* 18.2195 balances only after a calculated surplus of 200 artabas has been conceded "to the farmers of Euangelion and others on the orders of our master,"[27] indicating that the surplus was used for a purpose other than paying the *embole*.

---

20. On the *embolator*, see *P.Oxy.* 56.3873.8 n.; Hardy 1931, 57; Johnson and West 1949, 327. In *P.Oxy.* 18.2195, the account balances after the surplus is given away κα(τὰ) κέλευσιν τοῦ δεσπό(του) ἡμῶν.
21. *P.Oxy.* 55.3804.273, 16.1911.209, 18.2195.146.
22. On *adaeratio* and the levels of the *embole*, see the section titled "*Adaeratio*" below.
23. The cash for such remissions was presumably drawn from payments of money tax, like that Stephanous is to pay to the *embolator* in *P.Oxy.* 1.126.
24. Two lines from this account were given in the introduction to *P.Oxy.* 18.2196.r. The text is slated to be published in an upcoming volume of the *P.Oxy.* series. Hickey 2008 provides a detailed description and preliminary discussion of the document, providing many of the figures it contains. It should be noted, however, that two numbers have been transposed in the figure for *solidi* in line 1 of the fourth section. That figure is given as 13,451; it ought to read 13,541.
25. Hickey 2008, 90.
26. Hickey 2008, 90.
27. τοῖς γεωρ(γοῖς) Εὐαγγελίο(υ) καὶ ἄλλοις κα(τὰ) κέλευσιν τοῦ δεσπό(του) ἡμῶν.

The other possible explanation offered by Hickey is that the dues for the *embole* were paid in part or in total through *adaeratio* and were therefore grouped with the *argyrika* as money taxes. Yet the *analomata argyrika* in the higher-level account, unlike the *analomata* of the *pronoetes* accounts, exclude the expenses handled locally at the lower administrative levels.[28] Unlike other taxes, payment of the *embole* in kind was treated as a local expense handled at the level of the *pronoetai*, and we should therefore not expect to see the tax expenditures in grain in the higher-level accounts. Moreover, it is apparent from *P.Oxy.* 16.1911 and 16.1914 that grain in surplus of the *embole* was traded to the *embolator* for cash, which was then handed to the *trapezites* and, from there, to the higher administrative levels. There are no examples in which surplus grain is passed from *pronoetai* to higher-level administrators, who appear to have dealt strictly in cash;[29] that is, above the level of the *pronoetes*, any grain surpluses would have already been transmuted into cash, so there was no grain to be expended at the higher levels. This observation raises the question of why *lemmata sitou* (absent from *P.Oxy.* 16.1918.v) appear in *P.Oxy.* 19.2196.v at all. The *lemmata sitou* of the *pronoetes* accounts are, as noted above, gross receipts, exclusive of the various remissions and expenditures. If, as Hickey reasonably supposes, there is no reason to suspect that the *lemmata sitou* figures of the higher-level accounts are any different, it is especially curious that this figure, which bears little relation to anything that the higher-level administrators would have received or that the *pronoetai* would have paid out, should appear in *P.Oxy.* 18.2196.v.[30] One possibility is that the estates' fiscal obligations were determined based on the total target *lemmata sitou*, but a firm answer, if one can be given, might have to wait until the full publication of *P.Oxy.* 18.2196.v, which, to date, has only been described.

Kankellos *and* Metron *Artabas*

While the *pronoetai* write that the grain accounts balance, a closer comparison of grain receipts to grain expenditures complicates in what sense they are "balanced." The standard unit of dry measure in Egypt was the *artaba*, whose unit

28. Hickey 2008, 94.
29. This is true even under Sarris' administrative structure, which makes the *embolator* an estate employee (Sarris 2006, 79, fig. 5). The *embolator* receives grain, not money, from the *pronoetai*.
30. Hickey 2008, 90.

of subdivision was the *choinix*. Artabas of several different names appear in the Apion dossier and other contemporary papyri, and the most significant in the accounts are the *metron* and the *kankellos*. The measure for wheat on the receipts side of the accounts is usually the *metron artaba*,[31] whereas that for the expenditures is the *kankellos artaba*. At the end of the receipts section of *P.Oxy.* 55.3804, at the point where the sum of the collections is given, the scribe converts from *metron* to *kankellos* artabas and describes the method of conversion: σίτ(ου) μέτρ(ῳ) (ἀρτάβαι) Ατιβ δ´ χο(ίνικες) ε, αἳ κ(αγκέλλῳ) (ἀρτάβαι) ἐξ (ἑκατοστῶν) (ἀρτάβαι) ιε κ(αγκέλλῳ) (ἀρτάβαι) Αφθ δ´ χο(ῖνιξ) α.[32] This compressed phrase reads "1312¼ artabas by *metron* and 5 *choinikes* of wheat, which by *kankellos* at 15 per 100 are 1509¼ artabas 1 *choinix*." In other words, converting *metron* to *kankellos* entails adding 15 percent to the *metron* figure.[33]

The nature of the relationship between these two types of *artaba* is not entirely clear, though the possibilities are limited. The conversion may be from a larger measure to a smaller one; that is, the amount of grain may be the same, but the units into which it is divided may be different. This possibility could entail either a system with artabas of varying capacities containing different numbers of *choinikes* of a fixed size or a system of *choinikes* of varying capacities that make up artabas of similarly varying sizes.[34] Alternatively, the "conversion" could be explained as an actual difference in quantity of units of the same size. Strictly speaking, the difference in the measures, then, would be not a conversion but inclusive or exclusive of a surcharge.

If the *metron artaba* and the *kankellos artaba* both contain the same number of *choinikes*, varying artabas with fixed *choinikes* can be eliminated as a possibility. The editor of *P.Oxy.* 55.3804 points to several items in the account that demonstrate clearly that the *kankellos artaba* has 40 *choinikes*.[35] The question of the number of *choinikes* in the *metron artaba* has been more vexed. The editors of many of the early *P.Oxy.* volumes assumed that the *metron* had 46 *choinikes*, 15 percent more than the 40 *choinix kankellos*. But in *P.Oxy.* 16.1911.101–2, 14 *metron* artabas are converted to 16 artabas *kankellos* and 4 *choinikes*.[36] Based on this calculation, Shelton has argued that the *metron* also

---

31. This is not a rule. *P.Oxy.* 55.3084.148 is an exception, as is the corresponding entry *P.Oxy.* 16.1911.75. *P.Oxy.* 18.2195 has numerous *kankellos* entries on the receipts side.
32. *P.Oxy.* 55.3804.141–42.
33. On this conversion, see the highly detailed note to lines 141–42 in the commentary to *P.Oxy.* 55.3804.
34. The view that the sizes are fixed is expressed by Duncan-Jones (1979, 347–75, especially 361–69) and Mayerson (2006). The argument for variable sizes is made by Shelton (1977; 1981, 102–6).
35. The case is made in the note to lines 141–42. The editor points to lines 173, 177, 180, and 181.
36. σίτ(ου) μέτρ(ῳ) (ἀρτάβαι) ιδ, αἱ κ(αγκέλλῳ) (ἀρτάβαι) ἐξ (ἑκατοστῶν) (ἀρτάβαι) ιε. καγκ(έλλῳ) ἀρτάβαι) ις χο(ίνικες) δ.

contains 40 *choinikes*: "Fifteen percent of a 40-choenix artab is 6 choenices. Multiply by 14, 84 choenices. Divide by 40, 2 artabs with 4 choenices left over. Add to 14 artabs *metron*, total 16 artabs 4 choenices *kankellos* as stated. This is plainly the scribe's method of calculation, and it requires that both artabs, *metron* and *kankellos*, consist, each in its own system, of 40 choenices. Forty-six will not do."[37] Shelton then offers three other examples in which the *metron artaba* appears, by similar method of calculation, to consists of 40 *choinikes*: *P.Oxy.* 16.1910.18–27, 2037.24–25, and 18.2195.99–101. The editor of *P.Oxy.* 55.3804 notes, however, that "one may reach a perfectly satisfactory conclusion on the hypothesis of artabas of 46 and 40 choinices: choen. 644 (14 × 46) ÷ 40 = kank. art. 16 choen. 4."[38] Shelton is simply performing operations in a specific order, one that is not clearly preferable to any other.

The fourth column of *P.Oxy.* 55.3804, in which all the figures for the grain entries as well as the scribe's column subtotal are extant, can answer definitively the question of whether the *metron* has 40 or 46 *choinikes*. The column is unique in that the individual entries are given in *metron* artabas and *choinikes*, whereas the subtotal is given in whole and fractional *metron* artabas. In the column, there are four entries of 31.25 artabas and 5 *choinikes* and one entry of 3 artabas. This totals to 128 artabas and 20 *choinikes*, which the scribe notes as 128½ artabas. Half a *metron artaba* is clearly equated with 20 *choinikes*, so the *metron* artaba, like the *kankellos* artaba, consists of 40 *choinikes*. Varying artabas with fixed *choinikes* can therefore be eliminated. The possibility remains that the *choinikes* themselves varied in capacity but always represented one-fortieth of an *artaba*, regardless of that *artaba's* size. Were that the case, we should still expect to find a consistent ratio between conversions of *metron* and *kankellos* artabas. While a ratio of 1.15:1 is common, it is not consistently so, and a number of different ratios can be found in the papyri.[39] Further, Duncan-Jones notes that in *P.Cair.Zen.* 1.59004.14–16, an *artaba* is explicitly stated to contain 40 *choinikes*. He points out that if its capacity in *choinikes* had to be mentioned, it could not simply be assumed, which militates against the idea that a *choinix* means one-fortieth of an artaba regardless of the artaba's *size*.[40]

37. Shelton 1977, 59.
38. *P.Oxy.* 55.3804.142 n. The editor is not arguing in favor of a *metron equal to 46 choinix* but merely pointing out the flaw in Shelton's reasoning.
39. E.g., *P.Oxy.* 16.1910, 16.2027; *P.Iand.* 63. The editor of *P.Oxy.* 55.3804 has suggested that the varying ratios represent varying rates of surcharge. This possibility is discussed further below.
40. Duncan-Jones 1979, 368 n. 19. See also 369 nn. 25–33. I do not argue that all artabas were of 40 *choinikes*, only that both the *metron* and *kankellos* were. This argument should also be considered in light of the much earlier date of *P.Cair.Zen.* 1.59004, in the third century BCE.

This leaves as the most likely explanation for the conversions the second alternative mentioned above, that the 15 percent added to the figures in the accounts represents an actual addition of uniformly sized units to the number collected. If this is right, the *pronoetai* accounts show that the *pronoetes* collected rents from lessees and taxes from both lessees and independent smaller landholders, then expended that amount plus an additional 15 percent on wages, payments, donations, and taxes, in order to balance the accounts. Attempting to explain the purpose of this additional 15 percent, the editor of *P.Oxy.* 55.3804 has argued that *metron* and *kankellos* are "accounting terms only, the former implying 'exclusive of surcharges,' the latter 'inclusive of surcharges.'"[41] The editor points to Gascou's model and holds that in the case of the Apion estate, the surcharges are equivalent to the taxes collected by the estate on the state's behalf.[42]

P.Oxy. 55.3804 balances in grain precisely without the need to sell excess to the *embolator*, hence the grain surcharges paid out must appear in the expenditures of the account. The *embole* entry of line 149 is the lone tax payment made in the expenditures. Thus, on the editor's hypothesis (under which the surcharges are to be equated with the taxes), the entirety of the 15 percent surcharge should have been devoted to the *embole*. This hypothesis can be tested by determining whether the amount of the *embole* is equal to the difference between the *metron* and *kankellos* figures, that is, the 15 percent of the *metron artaba* figure added by the scribe.[43] The difference between the *metron* and the *kankellos* figures is 195.75 artabas and 6 *choinikes*, and the *embole* is 192.5 artabas and 7 *choinikes*, within .25 percent of one another compared with the *metron* total.[44] This small discrepancy between the figures may be attributable to methods of calculation used by ancient scribes generally and this scribe in particular.[45]

While the calculation works out well for this particular account, most of the

41. *P.Oxy.* 55.3804.141–42 n. That remissions on rent are calculated in *metron kankellos* artabas, the tax-inclusive term, indicates that the reasons for a remission in rent also occasioned a remission in the taxes owed on that land by the estate.
42. *P.Oxy.* 55.3804.141–42 n. (p. 128).
43. This figure is exclusive of the 26 *kankellos* artabas collected. Line 139 is the lone instance in *P.Oxy.* 55.3804 of a collection made in *kankellos* artabas. It is not included in the calculation of 15 percent for the *embole*, since, as the use of the term *kankellos* (surcharge included) indicates, it has already been supplemented with the 15 percent owed in taxes and, therefore, need not be taxed again.
44. 14.92 percent and 14.67 percent of the *metron* figure, respectively.
45. See 55.3804.141–42 n., on the occasional difficulty of determining how the scribe arrives at the numbers he does.

other *pronoetes* accounts are not sufficiently intact to determine as easily the *embole* figure or its relationship to the totals collected and expended. But where an idea of those numbers can be had, the picture is more complicated. *P.Oxy.* 16.1912 preserves the figure for grain *lemmata* converted to *kankellos* artabas (exclusive of the collections made in *kankellos* artabas), and the amount of the *embole* paid out, also in *kankellos* artabas. Under the editor's hypothesis, the *embole* figure should be 15 percent of the converted *lemmata* figure. In fact, it is more than 53 percent. In *P.Oxy.* 18.2195, the total collections for a tenth indiction are given in the text as 4,236¼ *kankellos* artabas and 6 *choinikes*, and the *embole* paid out is given as 3,585.25 *kankellos* artabas and 6 *choinikes*. The *embole* thus makes up nearly 85 percent of the total collections. But unlike *P.Oxy.* 55.3804 (where only one item of collection was given in *kankellos* artabas), a large number of the collections made in *P.Oxy.* 18.2195 are in *kankellos* artabas. These collections, like the 26 *kankellos* artabas collected in *P.Oxy.* 55.3804, would not have been subject to a second extraction of surcharges. Excluding the collections made in *kankellos* artabas reduces the number of *metron* artabas actually collected in the account to 2,819.5 plus 1 *choinix*. Converting this figure to *kankellos* results in 3,241.75 artabas and 7 *choinikes*, making the *embole* more than 110 percent of the entire *metron* collection.

Although the *embole* figure is missing from *P.Oxy.* 16.1911 and although the column where it would appear is lacunose in certain other areas as well, the column subtotal survives.[46] The extant expenditures recorded in that column are identical to the corresponding section of *P.Oxy.* 55.3804, being mostly customary remissions or church donations. The column's lacunose areas other than the *embole* can therefore be supplemented with some certainty using the figures from *P.Oxy.* 55.3804. Using those supplements, the *embole* figure in *P.Oxy.* 16.1911 can be recovered by subtracting the sum of all the entries in the column from the column subtotal given by the scribe.[47] This yields a figure of around 74 *kankellos* artabas for *embole* in 16.1911, or only about 5 percent of the *metron artaba* total, much less than the 15 percent in *P.Oxy.* 55.3804.

The situation was clearly not always so tidy as it appears in *P.Oxy.* 55.3804, and it is certainly possible that the *embole* there is equal to the 15 percent added in the conversion from *metron* to *kankellos* only because of happenstance. But the perspective we get from the *pronoetes* accounts is not that of the operators

46. Column iv, lines 76–77.
47. *P.Oxy.* 55.3804.168 n.

of the whole system. The appearance in the accounts of payments from one *pronoetes* to another and the fact that certain receipts are reckoned in *kankellos artabas*, practices that are perhaps related, imply a more complicated big picture.[48] It is possible that, seen from the bird's-eye view of the Apion bureaucrats in Oxyrhynchus and Alexandria, these differences offset one another in the aggregate, so that the average amount paid for *embole* by all of the Apion *pronoetai* was 15 percent on top of the total grain receipts. Such a system would have entailed very carefully constructed *apaitesima* in order to ensure that the aggregate numbers worked.[49] Texts like *P.Oxy.* 16.1918 and 18.2196.v, high-level accounts from the Apion estate, demonstrate that the higher levels of Apion administration did deal with aggregate numbers, operating from the bird's-eye perspective, rather than maintaining the *prostasia* divisions in their own accounts.

Adaeratio

Another complicating factor in comparing the amounts of *embole* paid in different accounts is the practice of *adaeratio*. Because, as noted above, money collected was dealt with at a level above that of the *pronoetes*, we do not find adaerated *embole* payments in the expenditures of their accounts. When *adaeratio* has occurred, however, we might expect a difference in the total amount of money passed along to the *trapezites* at the end of the account. In *P.Oxy.* 16.1911, where less grain is handed over for *embole* than in *P.Oxy.* 55.3804 (which covers the same *prostasia*), the amount of money given to the *trapezites* is greater by about 22 *solidi*. From the *pronoetes* accounts, it is impossible to determine how many of those 22 *solidi*, if any, were adaerated *embole* and how many were rents and money taxes. It is possible, however, to determine whether 22 *solidi* is sufficient to accommodate the adaeration of the artabas expected in *P.Oxy.* 16.1911, based on the 15 percent figure. In *P.Oxy.* 16.1909, a list of taxes from Oxyrhynchus, 10 artabas are equivalent to precisely 1 *solidus*. This gives a good approximation of the rate of *adaeratio* but does not specify either the

48. For example, a payment for the estate of Kephalas in *P.Oxy.* 18.2195.144 is added separately to the account's *lemmata*. On Kephalas, see also *P.Oxy.* 16.1916; Hickey 2008, 60 and n. 111.

49. A reluctance to make frequent changes to those carefully constructed documents can explain the accounting method that avoids altering the receipts based on them.

standard of the *solidus* or the type of *artaba*.[50] Johnson and West give a table of prices of wheat in *solidi* from the sixth century.[51] Several of the examples are instances of *adaeratio*, and most of those from Oxyrhynchus fall in the range of 9 to 13 artabas to the *solidus*.[52] Which *solidus* and which *artaba* are meant is not always mentioned, and the different rates might be attributable to this fact rather than indicative of actual variance in the rate of exchange. *P.Oxy.* 16.1907 is a remission of taxes that gives 9 1/6 *kankellos* artabas to the ὄβρυζον *solidus* and that also gives the equivalence of the ὄβρυζον to the Alexandrian standard.[53] The standard of *solidus* used in the *pronoetes* accounts is the private, but *P.Oxy.* 55.3804.150 gives the equivalence between the Alexandrian and the private. This works out to about 9⅓ *kankellos* artabas to the private *solidus*. In *P.Oxy.* 16.1911, the *pronoetes* hands over 118.5 fewer artabas of wheat to the boatmen than in *P.Oxy.* 55.3804, which, at 9⅓ artabas to the *solidus*, is equivalent to about 12.5 *solidi* and 5 *karats*. The 22 excess *solidi* in the surplus of *P.Oxy.* 16.1911 over that in *P.Oxy.* 55.3804 can therefore accommodate the adaeration of the *embole* absent from the grain expenditure in 16.1911.

While the relatively lower *embole* payment and higher money surplus in *P.Oxy.* 16.1911 could suggest that some of their dues in grain were indeed paid in money, in none of the *pronoetes* accounts is it explicitly clear that the estate paid in cash what it owed in grain. Given the long noted Apion preference for keeping gold rather than produce,[54] it would be counterintuitive if the estate had its *pronoetai* pay even part of its grain taxes in money, unless absolutely necessary. Nevertheless, in *P.Oxy.* 16.1911, a small surplus in grain does remain. This fact, which undermines the idea that part of the *embole* was adaerated, suggests that less was due or at least paid for *embole* in the year recorded by *P.Oxy.* 16.1911 than for that covered in 55.3804. The editor of *P.Oxy.* 55.3804 proposes, "This case seems to indicate rather that the Apions left themselves free to make up their quota of grain tax in whatever way best suited the particular current

50. *P.Oxy.* 16.1909.v gives different rates for unspecified artabas and solidi but is not internally consistent, and the arithmetic in it has problems.

51. Johnson and West 1949, 177.

52. There are outliers at *P.Oxy.* 16.1911.147–49 and 55.3804.184–85, in which 1 *solidus* is worth 24 *kankellos* artabas. As noted by the editor of *P.Oxy.* 55.3804 (184–85 n.), the higher value of the *solidus* may be due to the charitable nature of the transaction.

53. Ὄβρυζον, literally meaning "pure," refers to the wear of the soft gold *solidi* owing to circulation and use. When applied to coins going out of the imperial treasury, as in the case of *P.Oxy.* 16.1907, the term means that they have not been diminished. In the context of payments into the treasury, it refers to an additional per *solidus* fee meant to account for the diminution. See West and Johnson 1944, 132–33.

54. E.g., Hardy 1931, 100–101.

circumstances."[55] Alternatively, *P.Oxy.* 16.1907, a remission of a fourth of the grain taxes that had been paid, demonstrates that there were sometimes reductions of *embole* after the fact, and other sources record imperial remissions of taxes and perhaps increases as well.[56] The reluctance to alter the receipts side of the accounts meant that the *pronoetai's* target receipts remained unchanged during these occasional variations; instead, remissions on the expenditures side of accounts increased.

There are three possible explanations for the varying amounts of the *embole*: (1) the amount of *embole* paid for the *prostasia* in question remained the same but part of the dues were adaerated, (2) the total amount of *embole* owed by the estate remained the same but the amounts owed by the different *prostasiai* varied, or (3) the amount owed for *embole* occasionally varied but the target receipts remained unchanged. The second two options are likelier than the first. The extant examples of *adaeratio* in the Apion dossier are mostly remissions given to the payers rather than payments into the treasury or to the *embolator*, and the exceptions are complicated cases. *P.Oxy.* 1.127 (sixth century) is a list of *embole* payments made by the Apion estate. A cash payment made along with the *embole* is characterized by the editors as *adaeratio*.[57] This payment, obscurely called ὑ(πὲρ) τοῦ διαγράφου τοῦ τηγάνου,[58] is at a rate of 55½ *solidi* per 10,000 artabas, a rate far below any other attested rates of adaeration. It is more likely a fee or surcharge of some type. *P.Oxy.* 16.2020 shows the adaeration of grain related to the *arkarika*, the money tax that was to be paid along with the *embole* to the *embolator* in *P.Oxy.* 1.126. But the context of that account is very muddy. Column i, missing the first halves of its lines, describes the adaeration into *solidi* of a commodity (perhaps grain), for the *arkarika*. The name of what is being adaerated does not survive, but a payment of barley in kind is grouped with the adaerated entries, and only payments of barley in kind are present in the other two columns. The *arkarika* in *P.Oxy.* 1.126 was a money tax, explicitly contrasted with the *embole* to be paid in kind, always in wheat. There is no clear reason to connect the document with the adaeration of wheat for the payment of the *embole*. Indeed, it seems that the *embolator* was more in the business of giving money for grain than of accepting money in place of grain. When a re-

---

55. *P.Oxy.* 55.3804.158 n. Which particular circumstances would make it advantageous to the estate to hold on to grain and expend money are not immediately apparent.

56. See Hickey 2008, 95 with refs. in n. 35. On the remission of taxes, see *NJ* 148, 163.

57. *P.Oxy.* 1.126.9 n., referring to 1.127.2.

58. τηγάνον occurs here for τάγηνον, meaning usually "frying pan." Johnson and West (1949, 317) offer some conjectures on this puzzling usage.

duction of grain taxes was in order, grain was not returned to the payer, but the value of the grain in cash was returned; when there was a surplus of grain, it was handed over to the *embolator* in exchange for cash.[59]

Even if the *pronoetai* were not in the habit of making adaerated *embole* payments to the *embolator*, however, smallholders from whom they collected still could have adaerated their own payments to the estate. While it is impossible to say how much of a given *lemma* was adaerated, the accounts make clear that the dues collected from those associated with the estate were paid partially in cash. The *pronoetai*, however, paid out the *embole* in wheat to the greatest extent possible. In this way, the estates retained a greater proportion of money, effectively transmuting their own wheat collected as rent into gold, upon collection and payment of the estate's share of the grain taxes.[60] With this system in place, the estates were able to effectively "sell" their wheat collected as rent, without producing a surplus above their fiscal obligation or engaging in market-oriented commerce.

The following hypothetical example illustrates the system I posit: Let us say the estate collects 750 artabas of wheat in rent. It also collects 50 *solidi* from lessees as the adaerated value of 500 artabas, as well as another 250 artabas of wheat for taxes from those who pay their taxes through the estate. The estate owes 1,000 artabas of wheat in *embole*. From its pooled collections of both taxes and rents, it has 1,000 artabas and 50 *solidi*. The estate pays the *embole* entirely in wheat and is left with 50 *solidi* and no wheat. It has transmuted its 500 artabas of wheat into cash.[61]

Banaji has described estates like the Apions' as highly integrated into the monetary economy of Byzantine Egypt because of their ability to generate large amounts of gold.[62] He attributes this ability chiefly to their adoption of mechanical irrigation and the related expansion of the wine industry. Yet Hickey's studies have shown that the possibilities offered by capital investment and irrigation machinery are limited and that the estates were essentially autarkic, generating only enough wine to meet their own needs.[63] The system I describe can

59. E.g., *P.Oxy.* 16.1914, 1907.
60. This would also explain the inconsistent ratios of cash to kind in the collections *lemmata*: individuals who owed the same amount in rent, tax, or both adaerated different quantities of the wheat they owed.
61. See, further, figure 2, in chapter 4. This example would be accounted by the *pronoetes* as a balance in grain, with a cash surplus.
62. Banaji 1999, 205. See also Banaji 1996, 2000.
63. Hickey 2007, 302; 2001; 2012.

begin to disentangle the conflicting coexistence of a monetary economy and productive autarky on the estates. But if the estates were not selling their produce, the cash must have come from somewhere. The collection of adaerated sums from those paying taxes through and rents to the estate implies market engagement on the lower levels and another set of activities on the part of the *pronoetai*.[64] It is unlikely that the very small landholders and tenants would have been dealing in large denominations of gold *solidi*. Indeed, the appearance of *denarii* in their accounts confirms that the *pronoetai* dealt at least partly in billon. The process of transmuting that billon and kind into gold is another avenue by which the *pronoetai* and the estates stood to gain. This activity is discussed further below, in this chapter's section on the archive of Papnouthis and Dorotheos.

What Is the Source of the Extra 15 Percent?

If, as I argue, the accounts show that the *pronoetai* expended (or failed to collect) 15 percent more than they took in from collections, what was the source of that additional grain? An Apion *pronoetes* contract confirms that the *pronoetai* were personally responsible for obtaining it: "I further promise to credit to your magnificence, as compensation for the receiving measure, fifteen artabas on each hundred artabas."[65] The question of where a *pronoetes* obtained the extra 15 percent therefore arises. A *pronoetes*' ὀψώνιον (wage) is mentioned but not specified in *P.Oxy.* 1.136; in three *pronoetes* accounts, it is said to be a customary 24 artabas of wheat and 2 *solidi* less 5 carats for the year; and in two other accounts, the *solidi* are excluded while the artabas are the same.[66] This is not nearly enough to make up the 15 percent surcharge, especially given the further stipulation in *P.Oxy.* 1.136 that the *pronoetes* must pay the estate 12 *solidi* as a customary παραμυθία for the privilege of his post.

The disparity between a *pronoetes*' income and the financial obligations he had toward the estate points to some means of moneymaking activity outside the collections he made and recorded in the accounts. The editor of *P.Oxy.*

64. See figure 2, in chapter 4.
65. *P.Oxy.* 1.13627–29: προσομολογῶ δὲ λημματίσαι τῇ ὑμῶν ὑπερφυείᾳ ὑπὲρ παραμυθείας τοῦ παραλημπτικοῦ μέτρου τῶν ἀρταβῶν ἑκατὸν ἀρτάβας δέκα πέντε. For the identification of this clause with the conversion from *metron* to *kankellos*, see also *P.Oxy.* 55.3804.142 n. (p. 128).
66. *P.Oxy.* 55.3804.154, 16.1912.130, 18.2195.89; 19.2243a.81, 16.1910. No other amounts are attested.

55.3804 suggests that "the real emoluments of the office were the perquisites which the stewards could extract from the tenant farmers."[67] In *P.Oxy.* 19.2239 (598), a non-Apion contract of an *epikeimenos*, an estate overseer similar to a *pronoetes*, but with a wider purview, gives an idea of the type of perquisites a *pronoetes* might expect. In addition to his payment in money and kind, Ieremias, the *epikeimenos*, is entitled to "all the perquisites which the overseer is used to taking customarily from the farmers, either in wheat or wine or another form."[68] But like the *pronoetes* in *P.Oxy.* 1.136, Ieremias also must pay the estate a relatively large amount in *solidi* (30).[69] The contract in *P.Oxy.* 1.136 is for one year, and although the term is not stipulated in *P.Oxy.* 19.2239, the editor points out that Ieremias describes himself as already holding the position of *epikeimenos*. This type of payment, therefore, seems to have been not a onetime entrée but a due paid upon the renewal of each contract.[70] Clearly, the position was not a money loser for the *pronoetai* and *epikeimenoi*, so they must have been able to extract from the *georgoi* under them at least the amount to which they were liable to the estate, probably more.

From the perspective of the estate, this arrangement was essentially a way to extract more from its associated tenants and smallholders. The estate obtained a fixed annual income guaranteed by contracts with its *pronoetai* and other administrators, thereby transferring some of the risk at the cost of a smaller return. By assuming this risk, the *pronoetes* gained the opportunity to make money at the margins. A pair of petitions from *enapographoi georgoi* to their landlords show how this risk was pressed further down the social ladder, onto the shoulders of lessees. In the case of a minor disaster on a farm, the *pronoetai* or similarly charged administrators would still obtain their perquisites, even at the cost of ruin for the lessee. The first example is a late sixth-century petition in which an *enapographos georgos* explains to Apion II that he was forced to take out a sizable loan to replace dead livestock and would have to leave his land unless he received some relief. In the petition, the *georgos* complains that "my master's subordinates refused to act according to my good master's will" in re-

67. *P.Oxy.* 55.3804.154 n., relying on Gascou 1985, 17.

68. 19.2239.19–20: πάσας τὰς συνηθείας ἅς εἴωθεν λαβεῖν ὁ αὐτὸς ἐπικείμε(νος) κατὰ τὸ ἔθος παρὰ τῶν γεωργῶν εἴτε ἐν σίτῳ καὶ ἐν οἴνῳ καὶ ἐν ἄλλοις εἴδεσιν.

69. Whereas this payment was called a παραμυθία in *P.Oxy.* 1.136, it is an εἰσβατικόν here. The latter word appears only one other time in the papyri, in *P.Lond.* 2.393 (p. 333), in an obscure context. The editor of *P.Oxy.* 19.2239 (21 n.) believes that the two terms are equivalent in the context of the contracts.

70. The editor of *P.Oxy.* 19.2239 is ambivalent on this point. See the introduction and 21 n.

leasing him from his obligations.[71] In the second, a similar petition from a different *georgos* and probably also addressed to Apion II,[72] things have progressed further: the *enapographos georgos* asks to be permitted to return to his former *ktema* after three years of flight precipitated by the death of his livestock and his concomitant inability to pay what he owed. Without his animals, the *georgos* could not sow and therefore could not pay, which he said led to "the *pronoetes* coming onto the *ktema* and seizing all my meager belongings."[73]

The Archive of Papnouthis and Dorotheos

The contract clauses stipulating the obligation of the *pronoetai* to the estates include payment of gold *solidi* in addition to payment in grain. If the *pronoetai*'s means of obtaining this money is taken to be analogous with their means of obtaining grain, we should look to their relationship with the *georgoi* to discover the source of procuring that coin. Presumably the *pronoetai* could extract anything of value from the farmers to meet their obligations to the estate. That the estate required *solidi* from the *pronoetai* indicates a further level of activity, since the quantities noted in the contracts are far larger than those with which most *georgoi* would have been dealing. The *pronoetai* or, perhaps, those they dealt with must have been engaged in transmuting the quantities of billon and kind extracted from the *georgoi* into gold.

While it is difficult to know precisely what this activity entailed for the Apion *pronoetai* of the sixth century, evidence from earlier centuries can be illustrative. The fourth century in particular is important to understanding the subsequent three centuries, since it marks the beginning of the social, political, and economic changes that would come to define the epoch. Sarris has written that "the fourth century witnessed the consolidation of those centrally articulated and centrally focused 'tetrarchic' governmental institutions that transformed relations between the imperial authorities and provincial elites."[74] While Sarris' description of that transformed relationship differs from the one posited here, it is clear that the fourth century serves not only as a cultural touchstone,

71. *P.Oxy.* 1.130.14–16: οἱ διαφέροντες τοῦ ἐμοῦ δεσπότου οὐκ ἠνέσχετο ποιῆσαι κατὰ τὴν κέλευσιν τοῦ ἐμοῦ ἀγαθοῦ δεσπότου.

72. The *origo* of the *georgos* is the *epoikion* Kineas, known from *P.Oxy.* 16.1915 to have been administered by the Apions.

73. *P.Oxy.* 27.2479.21–22: ἐλθὼν ἐν τῷ κτήματι ὁ προνοητὴς διήρπαξεν πάντα τὰ εὐτελῆ μου πράγματα.

74. Sarris 2011, 256–57.

marked by the official acceptance of Christianity, but also as an economic one, marked by Constantine's introduction of the gold *solidus*, the economic foundation of the Byzantine world for centuries beyond the flourishing of the Apions. Papyri from the fourth century, often qualitatively different from the type of evidence predominating from the fifth through seventh centuries only by dint of survival, can therefore illuminate otherwise inaccessible aspects of the Apion estate.

An archive of the fourth century details the activities of Papnouthis and Dorotheos, two brothers engaged in the collection of rents and taxes in Oxyrhynchus on behalf of private employers and at least one *praepositus pagi*. The brothers provide a valuable model for conceiving of the activities of the Apion *pronoetai*. The archive of Papnouthis and Dorotheos comprises mainly letters detailing the business transactions involved in the collection of rents and taxes and the problems that arose for the brothers in the course of those dealings. The letters reveal precisely how collections of taxes and rents took place, information nearly absent from the Apion dossier. Significantly, the archive also indicates that the same individuals performed both public and private functions, perhaps at the same time.[75]

The system under which Papnouthis and Dorotheos operated in the collection of taxes entailed their purchasing the right to collect from the official in charge of collection for the amount that official owed.[76] The brothers would take out a loan in gold and sometimes silver at interest from a private lender for the amount owed by a particular locale.[77] The two brothers would then pay the official the full amount he was obliged to collect and be granted the right of collection.[78] The next step was the actual collection of taxes, which would have been made not in gold, since the small amounts owed by individual villagers would not have amounted to the value of a *solidus*, but in billon and even kind.[79] Converting this billon and kind into gold through market speculation was an area where collectors like Papnouthis and Dorotheos could hope to make a living. The price of gold could fluctuate on the order of 4 percent per year, enough to provide ample opportunity for profit.[80] In one letter, Dorotheos tells his

75. Bagnall (1993, 158–60) argues in favor of concurrence; Ruffini (2010) argues against.
76. Chapter 4 examines this activity in the broader context of ancient tax farming.
77. *P.Oxy.* 48.3394, 48.3393.13–15. For the interest, see *P.Oxy.* 48.3393.17–19, 48.3417.23–27
78. *P.Oxy.* 48.3393.5–9, 48.3419.
79. See the editor's introduction to *P.Oxy.* 48.3384–3429 (pp. 75–76.) See also Carrié 1993, 146–50; Bagnall 1993, 158–60.
80. Bagnall 1993, 159 n. 50.

brother of a particularly good price on gold and urgently requests that he send money to make the purchase before word of the deal spreads.[81]

Thus the occupation existed on the margins and involved the assumption of huge amounts of risk. Many of the letters in the archive detail the myriad ways in which things could go wrong. In addition to the risks involved in speculation, the brothers were exposed to double-dealing on the part of the officials responsible for paying the taxes. In one case in which the brothers purchased collection rights from the responsible official and attempted to collect, they learned that another collector had already been through. The official had apparently sold the rights twice. The brothers—now indebted to their original lender, without the collateral needed to take out another loan, and unable to collect the taxes they bid on—were petitioning for recourse against the contracting official, their social superior.[82] We do not learn how the brothers made out. Different letters describe villagers who paid in grain of substandard quality, others who were reluctant to pay, and others who outright refused.[83]

Some documents in the archive also show that Papnouthis was employed privately as a *pronoetes*, either concurrently or before he was engaged in tax collection.[84] How such private collections were carried out is not revealed with the same detail in these documents as in those concerning tax collection, but the basic responsibilities of the position were similar to those of the *pronoetai* of the Apion estate. Owing to the public and private aspects of the archive of Papnouthis and Dorotheos, Bagnall has argued that it represents the nascent blending of public and private that we see fully realized two hundred years later in the activities of the Apion *pronoetai*.[85] Ruffini has argued, however, that the notion of the Papnouthis and Dorotheos archive evincing a novel blending of public and private spheres is insufficiently supported.[86] He points out that the chronological evidence for the letters in the archive suggests a private phase followed by a public phase in the brothers' careers. He also notes that the letters documenting public activity and private activity cannot be definitively linked prosopographically. Rather than some novel blending of the public and private spheres, Ruffini sees in the archive a business-as-usual revolving-door system

81. *P.Oxy.* 48.3401. Papnouthis has confirmed a good price on gold.
82. *P.Oxy.* 48.3393, 3394.
83. *P.Oxy.* 48.3400.
84. *P.Oxy.* 48.3387–88, 3406–7.
85. Bagnall 1993, 159–60.
86. Ruffini 2010.

wherein private connections led to work in the public sector.[87] Ruffini's impression that this transition from private to public was a poor career move is surely influenced by the nature of the archive. Collections that went smoothly would not have warranted a letter and are thus underrepresented. Nevertheless, distinctions between the private and the public are clearly drawn in the fourth century for Papnouthis and Dorotheos, whereas they are not so clearly drawn for the *pronoetai* of the Apion estate. Although distinct, the two activities were still sufficiently similar that the same individuals could be used for both public and private collections in the fourth century. The archive therefore provides direct evidence for activities that look very similar to those suggested by the Apion dossier.

Ruffini rightly points out that the root of the many difficulties that the two brothers encounter is their lack of social capital, which led to their being pushed around without recourse by those above them and without consequence by those below them. In making private collections, they acted as the agents of landowners of a higher social standing. By trading on the prestige of their employers, they were less susceptible to such problems. In their public collections, however, the brothers were contracted by a public official, whose own obligation was met at the outset when the brothers paid him for the right of collecting. Thus the official had no reason to confer his status onto the brothers. Their middling position left them vulnerable to their superiors (e.g., officials selling collection rights twice) and impotent against their inferiors[88] (e.g., peasants refusing payment, paying in contaminated grain, and using improper measures).

Clearly troublesome for those who would collect taxes, such a system also became detrimental to the efficient collection of taxes when risks to collectors began to outweigh benefits. From this perspective, the transition to the system of the sixth century is a settling of tax collection in the sphere of those with the most social, economic, and political capital, large landholders like the Apions. Whereas the independent brothers, relative nobodies, could not bring any social sway to bear on those with whom they were dealing, the Apion *pronoetai*, whether collecting rents or taxes, were direct representatives of those with the most sway. Having these large landholders involved in collecting taxes was thus also in the best interest of the imperial government, which was seeking the steady flow of taxes from Egypt to Constantinople.

87. Ruffini 2010.
88. Ruffini 2010.

This interest leads to the question posed at the beginning of the chapter, whether it was through reward or compulsion that the imperial government persuaded large landholders to do their bidding. If the system at work in the Papnouthis and Dorotheos archive was subsumed into the system in place on the Apion estate, the moneymaking process that such collectors benefited from at the margins in the fourth century would also have been subsumed into the lower-level management of the estate. Indeed, the two points at which money could be made in the fourth-century system, the loan from the private lender to the collectors and the speculation in gold markets, were brought into the estate's favor in the sixth century. First, the additional 15 percent on grain and the flat fee in gold that the *pronoetai* had to pay the estate for the privilege of holding the position were functionally equivalent to the interest that Papnouthis and Dorotheos had to pay to the lender in the fourth century; the estate was compensated for the risk involved in temporarily alienating themselves from something of value, rights to rent and tax revenue, just as a banker extending a loan was.[89] Second, the Apion *pronoetai* would also have needed to transmute billon and kind into gold, engaging in the gold market in the process. The several gold payments made by the *pronoetai* to the *trapezites* over the course of the year may be seen as evidence of their engagement in this sort of activity. The increasing proportion of collections in money for both rents and taxes would have sweetened the proposition of taking over the role of rent and tax collections for the estates, since the opportunity for moneymaking at the margins would have likewise increased.

Scale[90]

Based on the entries in *P.Oxy.* 16.2032, an account of payments from several people, Hardy counted entries from *pronoetai* for twenty *prostasiai*, which Ruffini has convincingly revised down to sixteen.[91] This gives the minimum possible number of *prostasiai* administered by the Apion estate, though both Hardy and Ruffini allow that there could have been several more. Using the aggregate target *lemmata* from all the Apion *prostasiai* in *P.Oxy.* 16.1918 and

89. This is essentially rent-seeking behavior: the Apions were granted a government monopoly on tax collection and could therefore seek rents from those who wished to undertake the activity.
90. My forthcoming article in *BASP* 53 expands on the material presented in this section of this chapter.
91. Hardy 1931, 82; Ruffini 2008, 107. Some names and locations are repeated.

18.2196.v, along with the target *lemmata* from the extant *pronoetes* accounts (i.e., individual *prostasiai),* it is possible to estimate the total number of Apion *prostasiai.* From there, it is possible to take the amounts that each *pronoetes* needed to pay the estate each year for the privilege of collection—known from *P.Oxy.* 1.136, the *pronoetes* contract—and determine how many *solidi* the estate stood to gain from employing *pronoetai* in collecting taxes: total *lemmata* ÷ *pronoetes lemmata* = number of *prostasiai*; number of *prostasiai* × 12 *solidi* = *solidi* gained from *pronoetai* annually. Taking 15 percent of the target grain *lemmata* from *P.Oxy.* 18.2196.v, it is also possible to determine the total number of artabas the *pronoetai* contributed to the Apion estate on top of their mandated collections. These two numbers represent the intrinsic benefits that accrued to the Apions for their collection of taxes.

There are six *pronoetes* accounts for which the gross *lemmata* in wheat and money are extant or can be calculated. Because the ratio of wheat to gold in these collections is not consistent across the accounts (ranging from 2.3:1 to 11.3:1 in ratios of artabas to *solidi*), it is not possible to simply take either the grain *lemmata* or the money *lemmata* from the *pronoetes* accounts and compare them to the grain or money *lemmata* from the higher-level account. Instead, it is necessary to determine the value of the entire *lemmata* of a *pronoetes* account (cash and wheat combined) to see if a suitable paradigmatic number can be reached. Applying the *adaeratio* figure from *P.Oxy.* 16.1909 (10 *artabas* to the *solidus)* to the wheat *lemmata* in each of the *pronoetes* accounts and adding this to the cash *lemmata* yields the total value in *solidi* of the target collections for each of the *prostasiai* represented in the accounts. In five of the six accounts, dating from the 550s to the 590s, the value of the combined *lemmata* in *solidi* is quite consistent, between 750 and 830 *solidi*, with an average of just under 800 *solidi.*[92] We may say, then, that a *pronoetes*' target collection from a paradigmatic *prostasia* was valued at about 800 *solidi* per year. A similar total value can be determined for the aggregate target *lemmata* in *P.Oxy.* 18.2196.v, yielding an aggregate *lemmata* value of just over 29,400 *solidi.*[93] Dividing this total by the paradigmatic average gives a figure of about thirty-seven *prostasiai* in 586/7. There are no *lemmata sitou* figures in *P.Oxy.* 16.1908, the document most simi-

92. The outlier, at 517.25 *solidi*, is *P.Oxy.* 16.1914, whose figures came from the calculations determining the surplus at the end of the account (after deductions had already been made), so this number may be low. Cf. *P.Oxy.* 18.2195, 19.2243a. Including *P.Oxy.* 16.1914 drops the average to a comparable 750 *solidi*. The average, excluding either *P.Oxy.* 16.1911 or 55.3804 (since these accounts are for the same *prostasia),* remains essentially unchanged.

93. (108,816.5 *kankellos* artabas ÷ 10) + 18512 *solidi* + (191.75 *karats* ÷ 24).

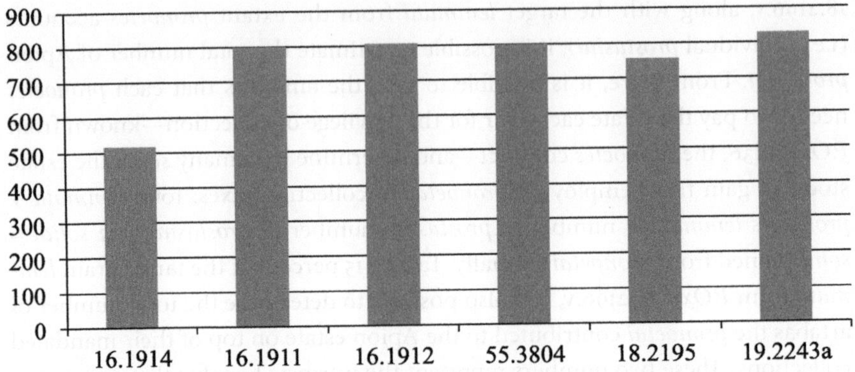

Fig. 1. The total value of the six extant *pronoetes* accounts, calculated using the *adaeratio* rate in *P.Oxy.* 16.1909

Table 1. Numbers from the six extant *pronoetes* accounts and the two extant estate-wide accounts, along with their total values in solidi

	Account		**Grain λήμματα**		**Money λήμματα**			**Ratio of**	**Total**
	Date	***P.Oxy.***	**Artabas**	***Choinikes***	***Solidi***	***Carats***	***Myriad denarii***	**artabas to *solidi***	**value in *solidi***
Pronoetes	556	16.1914.2–3	1,342	8	390.55	−180		3.50	517.25
accounts	557	16.1911.68–69	1,509.25	1	647.13		2,800	2.33	798.63
	566	16.1912.111–13	3,941.25	7	410.00		5,375	9.61	806.38
	566	55.3804.141–42	1,509.25	1	647.13		2,800	2.33	798.63
	576	18.2195.75–76	4,008.75	6	353.57		5,700	11.34	755.64
	590	19.2243a.59–67	3,245.25	2	507.85	−108	1,006	6.45	828.09
Estate-wide	542	16.1918.v 12			14,325.19				14,325.19
accounts	586/7	18.2196.v 31	108,816.5		18,512.00	191.75		5.88	29,401.64

Note: The total values were calculated using *adaeratio* rates from *P.Oxy.* 16.1909 of 10 artabas to the solidus. Fractions in the papyri are rendered as decimals to two places. Denarii are reckoned at 4,800 myriads to the solidus: see *P.Oxy.* 55.3804.272 n.

lar to *P.Oxy.* 18.2196.v, so its total value is equal to its cash *lemmata*, just over 14,325 *solidi*. This gives a figure of about eighteen *prostasiai* in 542.

Hickey has laid out several possible explanations for the significant increase in the money *lemmata* over the forty-five years between *P.Oxy.* 16.1908 and *P.Oxy.* 18.2196.v: investment and increased productivity (the position of Banaji and Sarris), the acquisition of more land, expansion of fiscal obligations (the number of people whose taxes the Apions collected), or increases in tax levels.[94] The *prostasiai* numbers above narrow the possibilities significantly. The calcula-

94. Hickey 2008, 99.

tion of the overall value of the *prostasiai lemmata* shows that their production levels were similar across data points spanning more than thirty years. Such stability in production indicates stability in the level of taxation as well, since tax increases would cause the *lemmata* per *prostasia* to rise.[95] Land acquisition and the expansion of fiscal obligations are the explanations left. If the two upper-level accounts are comparable, the number of *prostasiai* for which the Apion estate was responsible doubled over the course of forty-five years. The two estate-wide accounts, however, may not be strictly comparable, since grain figures are absent from the earlier *P.Oxy.* 16.1918.v. The more grain (if any) we assume was omitted from the earlier document, the more modest the level of expansion is by the time of the later document. But even if we assume that a collection of an amount of grain proportional to that in the later *P.Oxy.* 18.2196.v—a reasonable high-end estimate since ratios in the lower-level accounts do not trend either upward or downward over time—was omitted, for some reason, from the earlier account, there were still nearly a third more Apion *prostasiai* in 586/7 than there were forty-five years before.[96] Based on this analysis, the increase in the number of *prostasiai* associated with the Apion estate from the 540s to the end of the century falls in the range of 30 to 100 percent.[97] This increase tracks closely the surge in new Apion-associated toponyms that can be seen between the 540s and 590s.[98] The stability of the *lemmata* per *prostasia* further suggests that if the increase in overall *lemmata* is attributable to expanded fiscal obligation, it must have gone hand in hand with an increase in the number of *prostasiai* for which the Apions were responsible. Whether the *lemmata* from these additional *prostasiai* were predominantly from lessees or neighbors who paid taxes through the Apions is unclear, so the expansion of the fiscal obligations could certainly have made up the lion's share of the increase in *lemmata*.

The number of *prostasiai* for which the Apions were responsible also gives an idea of the intrinsic benefits of tax collection that accrued to the Apions. If the *pronoetes* contract of *P.Oxy.* 1.136 is taken to be standard, the estate could

95. Even if the estate reduced its rents proportionally to a tax increase, the collections of strictly tax from small landowners would have increased the total *lemmata* of the *prostasia*.

96. It is also possible that *P.Oxy.* 16.1918.v reflects total collections, with the grain having been wholly adaerated.

97. The sixteen προστασίαι in *P.Oxy.* 16.2032, consonant with the eighteen expected from the figures in *P.Oxy.* 16.1918.v before possible missing grain collections, makes the higher end of the range somewhat more probable.

98. Ruffini 2008, table 11 (p. 123), relying on data from Mazza 2001, table A (pp. 20–38). This rise cannot be attributed only to increasing numbers of documents from the period: see Ruffini 2008, table 10 (p. 122), relying on data from Mazza 2001, table A.

expect to receive 12 *solidi* in gold each year for each of the *pronoetai* it employed—215 *solidi* in 542, 444 *solidi* in 586.[99] Even more significant is the additional 15 percent of wheat the *pronoetai* would have contributed to the collections. The total amount of wheat to be collected by the *pronoetai* in 586/7 is more than 108,816.5 *kankellos* artabas.[100] Again, if *P.Oxy.* 1.136 is taken to be representative, the *pronoetai* contributed 15 percent of that figure, some 16,322 *artabas*, worth more than 1,632 *solidi* at the adaeration rate in *P.Oxy.* 16.1909. This gives the Apions a grand total in 586/7 of more than 2,073 *solidi* for the trouble of collecting their neighbors' taxes. This is about 7 percent of the estate's total target *lemmata* for that year.

Conclusion

The *pronoetes* accounts of the Apion estate record the collection of rents and taxes from tenants and independent smallholders and also the expenditures on estate expenses; provide the balance in cash and kind; and detail how surpluses were managed. In the accounting of grain by the *pronoetai*, the *metron* and *kankellos* artabas are used. The difference between the two is strictly one of accounting, the former being exclusive of extra charges, the latter inclusive. The use of these accounting terms implies the expenditure of more grain than was collected. While the most complete extant account, *P.Oxy.* 55.3804, suggests that this additional grain was for the *embole* payment, other accounts are harder to interpret. This difficulty of interpretation stems from the fact that the *pronoetes* accounts do not provide a system-wide perspective.

The practice of *adaeratio* further complicates an understanding of the accounts, but it can begin to explain the apparent contradiction of a monetized economy and productive autarky at work side by side. Because the estates collected both grain and money for both rents and taxes but prioritized paying taxes in grain, they were able to transmute their grain rents into money. Nevertheless, the contracts of the *pronoetai* show that they were personally responsible for acquiring this additional grain and were also obligated to give the estate a fixed amount of *solidi* annually for the privilege of the position. Because these obligations outstripped the wages of the *pronoetai*, they must have used

99. 12 *solidi* × 18 *prostasiai* = 215 *solidi* in 542; 12 × 37 = 440 in 586/7.

100. *Lemmata sitou* are absent from *P.Oxy.* 19.1918.v, so a similar figure cannot be calculated for the earlier period.

their position to extract the amount of their obligation and more, to make a living. Petitions from *georgoi* and contracts from positions similar to those of the *pronoetai* show that the extractions were made from the lessees and smallholders from whom the *pronoetai* made their collections.

The fourth-century archive of Papnouthis and Dorotheos provides details about a nascent form of the activities carried out by the Apion *pronoetai* and shows the process by which they could make money.[101] The archive comprises mainly letters detailing the business transactions of two brothers involved in the collection of rents and taxes, as well as the problems that arose in the course of those dealings. The difficulties the brothers encountered and mechanisms for forestalling similar difficulties in the later Apion system suggest a means by which large estates could have benefited from collecting taxes.

Finally, a quantitative comparison of the value of the *lemmata* of a paradigmatic *prostasia* to the value of the *lemmata* for the estate as a whole at points forty-five years apart in the sixth century demonstrates an increase in the number of *prostasiai* in that period on the order of 30 to 100 percent. This result indicates that the dramatic rise in gold *lemmata* during that period is attributable to the acquisition of more land or an expansion of fiscal responsibilities. The absence of evidence for expanding estates, however, points to expanded fiscal responsibilities as the likelier answer. The analysis also shows that the intrinsic benefits gained by the estate for the collection of their own and their neighbors' taxes amounted to about 7 percent of their total gross income. The relationship of this number to the scale of the extrinsic benefits (and therefore to total profits) is not available from the documents currently published. Potential sources of those extrinsic benefits, whatever their scale, are investigated in the next chapter.

101. Bagnall 1993, 158–60.

CHAPTER 4
Tax Collection on Two Tiers

The tax collection system in Oxyrhynchus under the Apions can be described as operating on two tiers. There were relationships between the collectors (e.g., the *pronoetai*) and the estate and between the estate and the imperial government.[1] In the previous chapter, a distinction was drawn between intrinsic and extrinsic benefits to the Apions from their tax collection activities. The papyri from Oxyrhynchus provide a great deal of evidence for evaluating the intrinsic benefits at the lower levels of Apion administration and the variety of ways in which the estate stood to gain from drawing money and produce upward. But the processes by which the Apions derived extrinsic benefits from their fiscal relationship with the government—not drawn upward from the rural peasantry, but flowing downward from the imperial government—did not leave behind a comparable record in the papyri or the literary sources.

This absence is most obviously owed to the provenance of the surviving papyri, Oxyrhynchus, which is not where most records of the high-level dealings were kept. We simply do not have anything like the Papnouthis and Dorotheos archive or the Apion *pronoetes* accounts detailing the inner workings of the state-estate relationship. The lack of direct evidence is the main stumbling block to examining the nature of the extrinsic benefits reaped from the Apions' collection of taxes. In the absence of direct evidence, then, it should prove use-

1. When writing of relationships with the "imperial government," I do not wish to imply anachronistic notions of strict central planning or budgets. Indeed, the local nature of tax collection and disbursements and the informal aspects of much of the fiscal apparatus are essential to the model proposed in this chapter and the following one. These relationships were personal ones between the Apions and the imperial family or functionaries or arrangements that the Apions themselves, as members of the imperial bureaucracy, made for their own personal enrichment.

ful to have a model that can describe the various social and economic circumstances influencing which system of tax collection emerges. This chapter offers a theoretical framework laying out the different possible systems of tax collection on the estate (at both the upper and lower tiers), describes the social and economic circumstances associated with each of these systems, and evaluates which system best suits the circumstances apparent in Byzantine Egypt.

Certain ideas from academic economics and sociology will be brought to bear here on the economy of late antique Egypt. It is therefore necessary to counter objections to the application of concepts from these disciplines to the ancient world.[2] Sarris' comments can stand in for the broader arguments against this type of analysis: "Unsatisfactory have been the attempts to impose wholesale on the ancient economy the latest fashions in academic economics, such as the so-called 'New Institutional Economics.' This can have the effect of reducing all past economic history to the glibly comparative language of business studies, generating largely ahistorical discussion of 'firms,' 'rent-seeking activity' and such like. As the financial crises of the early twenty-first century have revealed, liberal economists have problems getting to grips with modern capitalist society: it seems unlikely that they should have much to offer by way of insight into the ancient or medieval worlds."[3]

A few points can be made in response to these claims. First, it is possible to apply aspects of modern economic theories to ancient economies without imposing them wholesale. Second, unsuccessful application of ideas from one area of modern academic economics to ancient economies does not preclude successful application of ideas from any area of modern economics. Third, the mere fact of a phenomenon not being named or recognized in the past does not mean that the phenomenon did not exist or that the application of the modern

2. The bibliography on this subject is vast. The starting point of the modern formulation is Finley 1973 and 1999 (= 1973 updated and revised), arguing against the applicability of certain economic theories to the ancient world. Lyttkens (2010, 505 n. 1) offers a concise justification of economic analysis in ancient history: "The use of economic analysis in this context has been criticized on the grounds that economic life was 'embedded' in antiquity so that market forces played no independent part. This arguably is a matter of degree. On the one hand, much economic behaviour in the modern world is also 'embedded,' so the ancient world was not that different. On the other hand, embeddedness leaves considerable scope for analyses based in institutional economics, which emphasizes social norms, interaction between economic and social domains, and people's beliefs." For another evaluation of the terms of the debate, see Morris 1994, written twenty years after Finley's Sather lectures on which his 1973 book was based. Lyttkens (2013, *passim* and 6–13 especially) defends the use of certain economic theories, particularly new institutional economics.

3. Sarris 2011, 259. Ronald Coase's 1991 Nobel Prize speech, "The Institutional Structure of Production," offers a primer on the intellectual basis of new institutional economics.

label that has been given to the newly recognized phenomenon is ahistorical. Finally, the fact that modern economic theories sometimes failed to predict future events does not mean that they cannot accurately describe events of the past. To be sure, there are limitations to the approach, the most significant being that it does not readily admit of quantitative analysis—for example, determining the scale of the benefits to the estate from its arrangements on the upper tier. Still, applying concepts from economics permits a narrowing of the range of relationships that the Apions are likely to have had with the imperial government and can point in the direction of candidates suitable for historical analogy, the subject of the next chapter.

Investigations into methods of tax collection in different periods and places have revealed three broad headings under which relationships between the state and the collectors fall: share, rent, and wage.[4] Under a share system, the actual collections are counted, and a predetermined proportion of those collections go to the collector. Under a rent system—often referred to as tax farming—a collector pays some portion of the anticipated collections to the state, which grants him the exclusive right of collection. The collector keeps, as his compensation, any residual collected beyond the amount paid to the state. In wage systems, the collector's compensation depends not on the amount collected or expected to be collected but on the level of effort expended in collecting taxes. Thus an agreed-on salary is paid for the service of collection, and all collections are handed over to the state.[5]

Each system relies on the state measuring a different cost associated with collecting the taxes: counting the actual collections after the fact (revenues), estimating anticipated collections accurately before the fact (the tax base), and monitoring the efforts of collectors. Which system of collection emerges depends on the relative magnitude of these three costs. If actual revenues are easier to measure than either the tax base or the effort of collectors, share agreements are the norm. If it is comparatively easy to measure the tax base, rent agreements predominate. If the efforts of the collectors can be easily and reliably monitored, the wage model emerges. The

4. Azabou and Nugent 1988; Coşgel and Miceli 2009. The term *rent* is used *sensu lato* in this chapter, to refer to agreements in which the rights to something of value are handed over for a given period in exchange for money. In this case, the right to collect taxes is the thing of value. To avoid ambiguity, the word *lease* (rather than *rent*) will be used to refer to the specific type of rent agreement in which money is paid to a landowner for the use of land.

5. Coşgel and Miceli 2009.

relative magnitude of these three costs are, in turn, influenced by a number of social and economic circumstances, observed in a variety of historical milieus and outlined by Coşgel and Miceli. Their model essentially establishes the causal link for the correlated sets of circumstances and collection systems. Therefore, wherever a set of circumstances can be observed, the correlated system of collection is implied. Operating on the assumption, set out in chapter 3, that the Apion estate would not collect taxes absent some reward or compulsion, the model can be useful in evaluating a relationship for which there is little direct evidence, as is the case for the relationship between the Apions and the imperial government. In the presence of a certain set of social and economic circumstances, we can expect that one or another of the types of relationship is more probable to emerge. Determining which set of circumstances most closely aligns with those observable in Byzantine Egypt can point to which type of relationship is most likely to have emerged there. The more fragmentary or obscure evidence from the Apion dossier can then be interpreted more clearly in light of the implied relationship. I conclude in this chapter that the evidence and correlative circumstances point to a rent system for the Apion estate.

Testing the Model

Because the system governing the relationship between collector and state is readily apparent from the evidence in the archive of Papnouthis and Dorotheos, that archive can serve as an instructive test case for whether Coşgel and Miceli's model is applicable to late antique Egypt. Letters in the archive state explicitly that the brothers borrowed a certain amount, handed that over to a representative of the state, then made their collections and kept any excess for themselves—a clear example of the rent system. Coşgel and Miceli observe that a rent relationship is preferred when a tax is difficult to count due to the inconsistent suitability of the produce involved (since this raises the costs of counting revenue and monitoring collectors);[6] in *P.Oxy.* 48.3400, Papnouthis complains that he has found barley contaminating a village's wheat contributions. They also note the difficulty posed by differing standards of measurement in the ar-

6. Coşgel and Miceli 2009, 411.

eas of collection;[7] in that same letter, Papnouthis expresses doubts that the measure used by the inhabitants of the village is actually equal to the *kankellos demosios* measure they were using.[8]

A rent relationship is also preferred if the size of the tax base is particularly variable, because the risk under a rent system, in contrast to a wage or share system, is conferred to contracted collectors. A state can therefore still expect to receive a predictable level of revenue regardless of fluctuations from year to year. Coşgel and Miceli point to a number of external factors that increase the variability of a tax base, including inflation, population changes, and political upheaval.[9] All of these are prominent features of the so-called crisis of the third century. Runaway inflation is evident in the Heroninus archive after about 270 CE and was only resolved in Egypt after Constantine's introduction of the gold *solidus* around 310.[10] Precise population figures are notoriously difficult to come by for the late Roman Empire, even in Egypt, where censuses were taken every fourteen years until the end of the third century.[11] Still, even in the fourth century, Egypt was recovering from the Cyprian plague of the previous half century, which may have seriously affected the population there.[12] The fifty years of disarray between the reigns of Severus Alexander and Diocletian, when at least fifty-one different people were called emperor, have been characterized as "among the most disruptive ever experienced by the Roman Empire."[13] The archive of Papnouthis and Dorotheos comes then in the wake of a period of extremely high volatility. Under these circumstances, Coşgel and Miceli's model predicts that tax collection would have occurred under a rent system, which the direct evidence from the Papnouthis and Dorotheos archive confirms. The method I propose in examining the aspects of the Apion estate for which direct evidence is lacking is to work backward, identifying the circumstances conducive to a particular system of collection on each tier.

7. Coşgel and Miceli 2009, 411.
8. While the *metron* and the *kankellos* artabas appear to have measured the same volume (at least by the fifth century), there were other types of *artaba* as well, including the *mega metron* and *micron metron*, which do appear to have been local measures.
9. Coşgel and Miceli 2009, 413.
10. Rathbone 1991, 5 and appendix 2.
11. Corbier 2005, 398. See also Bagnall and Frier 1994.
12. Corbier 2005, 398. See also Tate 1992, 300–301. On the epidemiology of the Cyprian plague, see Conrad 1981, 70–71.
13. Drinkwater 2005, 28.

The System of Collection on the Lower Tier

That Apion *pronoetai* received an annual salary and handed over their collections suggests a wage model. Yet they paid the estate at a predetermined level, plus a premium for the privilege of collecting,[14] and, as I argued in chapter 3, they used their position both to provide themselves with capital for speculation and to extract from the peasantry what they could over and above the amount required by the *apaitesima*. Such behavior is much more characteristic of the rent model, wherein collectors "recoup their investments and make a profit on what they are legally entitled to collect—and often on what they can get away with collecting beyond that."[15] There is evidence that the Apion estate was accustomed to enter into rent contracts for collection of revenues other than taxes. *P.Oxy.* 58.3958 is a contract between the estate and a collector of urban rents in Oxyrhynchus. The collector is to pay the estate 125 *solidi* for the right to collect from some of the estate's urban holdings, that is, on a rent contract. The hybrid practice of the *pronoetai* is perhaps a vestige of the system, similar to that which Papnouthis and Dorotheos operated under, wherein the private functions of the fourth-century collectors (wage laborers) were distinct from the operations of the tax collectors (rent contractors). The minuscule level of wage payment to the Apion *pronoetai* compared to the annual fee they were obligated to pay the estate is evidence of the predominance of the rent model in their relationship with the estate.[16] Therefore, as the tax collection responsibilities began to fall under the purview of the *pronoetai*, the wage aspect of their employment took on a secondary role. Alternatively, the wage was used to provision the *pronoetai* over the course of the year, while their capital was tied up in illiquid investments.

As Papnouthis and Dorotheos did with the state and as the urban collector did with the estate, the Apion *pronoetai* maintained a rent contract relationship with the Apions. The rent charged to the *pronoetai* by the estate was the value of the *apaitesima*, minus remissions, plus the annual contracted money payment and an additional 15 percent on wheat. Their compensation rested on the possible extraction of further collections—the perquisites discussed in chapter 3—

14. The premium mentioned is the 12 *solidi* and 15 percent on grain collections stipulated in the *pronoetes* contract *P.Oxy.* 1.136.
15. Levi 1988, 72.
16. For the wage, see *P.Oxy.* 55.3804.154, 16.1912.130, 18.2195.89; for the annual fee, *P.Oxy.* 1.136.

and the availability of capital for speculation.[17] Unlike Papnouthis and Dorotheos, the *pronoetai* of the Apion estate did not borrow money up front to pay the estate in advance, instead paying their money collections in installments after the fact.[18] While not the usual arrangement, other historical instances of the rent model are consistent with installment payments that rent contractors made to the state only after collections had been made, like those made by the Apion *pronoetai*.[19] Installments paid after partial collection still diminished variance and, at the same time, allowed the estate and the *pronoetai* to benefit from speculation in gold. Moreover, because lower-tier collections were made using a rent system, the upper tier was insulated from variance in the tax base on the local scale (e.g., crop failure, damage to levies). The terms of the arrangement between the upper tier and the imperial government could therefore operate under terms consistent with low-variance circumstances; that is, the use of the *pronoetai* as subcontractors on rent contracts shifted the risks of variance to the lower tier. In doing so, the estate was able to ensure a relatively stable revenue stream from the rents and taxes for which they had collection rights.

Under such a rent system, the *apaitesima* and *pronoetes* accounts look like an attempt to estimate the tax base. The apparent invariability or "fossilization"[20] of these documents, at least during the nine years between *P.Oxy.* 16.1911 (557) and 55.3804 (566),[21] might seem to indicate that the variability of the tax base had diminished by the sixth century. The accounting practices discussed in chapter 3, however, likely mask what variability there was, since failures to collect were reflected in the expenditure portions of the *pronoetai* accounts. In the absence of a mechanism to account for increases in collection relative to the *apaitesimon*, those documents would have been the high-end estimates of anticipated revenue. It appears that estimations of the tax base changed significantly over the longer term, as reflected in higher-level accounts such as *P.Oxy.* 18.2196.v and 16.1918.v, which are separated by some forty years.[22] The virtual monopoly that the Apions had on collections

17. The 15 percent on wheat and the annual payment were ways for the estate to benefit from the perquisites available to the *pronoetai*.
18. See, e.g., *P.Oxy.* 16.1911, 55.3804.
19. Kiser 1994, 301.
20. Hickey (2008, 90 n. 12) uses the term *fossilized*.
21. I am assuming that the *lemmata* portions of the accounts are reflective of the *apaitesima*.
22. Hickey 2008. But even if the amelioration of the problems of inflation and political instability by the sixth century diminished variability of the tax base, other advantages offered by a rent system might have led to its persistence. The persistence of rent systems due to the other beneficial features they offer is discussed further in chapter 5 in the present study.

in their area of responsibility would have complicated setting the price for collection each year.[23] In situations without a competitive auction to set the bidding price, an earlier year's collections set the standard for subsequent years. The *pronoetes* accounts and the related *apaitesima* were therefore more probably attempts to estimate the tax base relative to previous years, a repurposed vestige of a collection system of earlier centuries, rather than a close accounting of collections to ensure the reliability of the collectors. Indeed, an attractive feature of a rent system is that there is no need to monitor collectors once the contracted payment has been received.

Coşgel and Miceli also note that the cost of measuring the tax base is reduced when an established system of accounting is in place.[24] This is why, they argue, rent contractors have historically been employed to collect taxes from larger enterprises, where bookkeeping permits accurate estimation of production and therefore the appropriate level of taxation, rather than from small shops, for which such estimates are more difficult.[25] Once incorporated into its tax collection apparatus by the Apions, the carefully accounted private collection system would have been conducive to the development of a rent collection system in the transition from the fourth century to the sixth.

The System of Collection on the Upper Tier

The taxes collected by the lower administrative tier of the Apion estate and handed to the upper tier were passed along, at some point, to the imperial government, again on the basis of either a share agreement, a rent agreement, or a wage agreement.[26] It is not necessarily the case that the upper and lower tiers operated on the same system. There have been multitiered systems in which a bureau overseeing collectors operating on one system operated un-

23. When a contract is likely to be awarded to a contractor on land over which he previously held collection rights, the scenario can be described as virtual monopoly on collection. In such cases, some means other than a competitive auction must be used for setting the price. Land surveys, censuses, and using previous years' collections as a baseline are all methods used in other historical contexts. I mean to imply not that the Apions had such a virtual monopoly on all Oxyrhynchite collections but only that the *apaitesima* represent use of a previous years' collections as a baseline for estimation of the tax base.

24. Coşgel and Miceli 2009, 412.

25. Coşgel and Miceli 2009, 412.

26. Money being fungible, it is not necessarily the case that collections from one year were handed to the state in that same year. It will be argued here that payment in anticipation of collection was an important part of the arrangement between the upper tier and the state.

der a different system and was monitored by another tier on still another system.[27] In *P.Fay.* 34 (161 CE), Heron buys the right to collect certain taxes from a pair of *boethoi* (the very title Papnouthis carried in his tax-collecting capacity), who were themselves contracted to collect. Heron makes reference to former years as precedent for the agreement, indicating that the practice was not uncommon.[28]

The *pronoetai* collecting taxes on the lower tier of the Apion administration were essentially subcontractors like Heron was in the second century, and the set of circumstances directing their relationship with the estate was different from the set dictating the relationship between the estate and the state. The circumstances that made the rent system most attractive on the lower tier were the relatively low cost of estimating the tax base and relatively high costs of monitoring collectors and counting revenue. One of the factors that Coşgel and Miceli observe as inflating the cost of counting revenue is the difficulty of counting collections in kind. As argued in chapter 3, by the time the Apion collections had been handed to the upper tier of administration, grain had been passed along for the *embole* or, along with billon, transmuted into gold. Therefore the problems associated with quantifying collections in kind were resolved, and the upper tier could deal with the state strictly in *solidi*. Finally, the relative monitoring costs may have been lower in the relationship between the upper tier of the Apion estate and the imperial government. Collections from the estates at this level were made by a full-fledged government bureaucracy that was more effective at monitoring and that required less monitoring itself.[29] Thus the factors making the rent system most attractive on the lower tier were absent on the upper tier. It cannot be assumed, then, that the relationship at the upper tier with the imperial government was also based on a rent contract simply because that was the system at the lower tier.

Even in the absence of these circumstances on the upper tier, the rent model would nevertheless have been attractive to the imperial government, by making capital available in the form of advance loans secured by future collections of taxes—a circumstance notably absent from the Apion *pronoetes* accounts. Kiser has noted the tendency of rent systems using small-scale distributed tax farmers, like Papnouthis and Dorotheos, to consolidate over time into larger and

27. Coşgel and Miceli 2009, 410. See also Kiser 1994, especially 294.
28. Wallace 1938, 290.
29. Coşgel and Miceli 2009, 414; Kiser 1994, 290 and *passim*.

larger syndicates.[30] He suggests that this phenomenon, observed in historical milieus as disparate as republican Rome and early modern France,[31] reflects a general trajectory of rent systems over time. Levi and Matthews argue that for Rome and France, this tendency stemmed from the role that tax farmers assumed as *de facto* central bankers, able to loan money to the government.[32] "Tax farming is as much a banking as a taxing system," Levi notes, because tax farmers possessed sufficient capital to advance money, secured by the right to collect from taxpayers, to the government.[33] As capital requirements of the government grew, the capital necessary to advance payments did as well; therefore, smaller tax-farming operations consolidated into larger ones. If collection in late antique Egypt followed a similar trajectory, the increasing importance of tax farming in making capital available to the imperial government led to the consolidation of small-scale collectors, of which Papnouthis and Dorotheos are an example in the fourth century, into sixth-century syndicates, similar to the colleges of landowners Gascou describes.[34]

Coşgel and Miceli point, however, to instances of rent contracts in which the collector himself took out a loan to cover the amount required by the government, as we see in the Papnouthis and Dorotheos archive, or in which payment was not advanced, as was the case for the Apion *pronoetai*. Such cases undermine both Levi's assumption that tax farmers needed to possess significant capital and Kiser's description of consolidation. In the former case, Coşgel and Miceli argue that the state could have simply gone to the same creditors as the collectors did in order to acquire capital on loan. But as Azabou and Nugent note, "since it had generally proved difficult for creditors to make sovereigns pay, until relatively recently the state . . . lacked the power to borrow on its own."[35] Because they could be pressed by private lenders, collectors like Papnouthis and Dorotheos served as a buffer between the state and those with money to lend. So while the collectors themselves did not possess much capital, they were an essential intermediary for the state to acquire capital on loan. In the case of the Apion *pronoetai*, money yet to be collected could, of course, not

30. Kiser 2003.

31. Levi 1988, 78; Matthews 1958, 36–42. These examples are discussed in detail in chapter 5.

32. Levi 1988, 77–78; Matthews 1958, 13–15.

33. Levi 1988, 77.

34. See chapter 1, n. 27, on the difficulty with the word *syntelestai*, which Gascou and others equate with these colleges. The existence of collection syndicates or of the phenomenon of prominent houses making collections is not, however, dependent on the identification that Gascou makes with *syntelestai*.

35. Azabou and Nugent 1988, 686.

be handed over. But the state's relationship was with the estate rather than directly with the *pronoetai*, so the availability of lending capital was only a matter of cash flow for the estate's upper tier.

Even if the use of rent contracts in tax collection did not arise and the collectors did not consolidate as a result of their ability to lend capital to the state, the availability of loans to the state could still have been a significant effect of it. In the sixth century, Justinian embarked on numerous wars of conquest that, aside from the inherent costs of warfare, sometimes also involved payments of large tributes. For instance, the peace with Persia negotiated in 561/2 had Constantinople paying out 30,000 *solidi* per year, with the first seven years paid up front.[36] This amounts to nearly 3,000 pounds of gold for the upfront payment and more than 400 pounds annually in subsequent years.[37] The government therefore certainly had an interest in acquiring gold in short order, increasing the value of a rent system able to provide advances on taxes. There was a limited level of agricultural capital investment possible for the Apions in Oxyrhynchus, and acts of munificence and lavish expenditure were legally constrained.[38] Acting as a creditor to the imperial government was one of the few uses of capital available to the Apions that would have generated returns.

As I argued in chapter 3, social factors also contributed to the transformation of the tax collection system from the fourth to the sixth centuries. The difficulties posed by the collectors' social status and the increased risk it forced them to assume made the business unattractive to small-scale collectors[39] and, therefore, to the imperial government, which could no longer reliably receive tax revenue or loans in anticipation of collection. The difficulties faced by Papnouthis and Dorotheos in the fourth century indicate that the risks were then beginning to outweigh the potential rewards.[40] Azabou and

---

36. Cameron 2000, 84. The terms of the settlement are given by Menander Protector (Blockley 1981, frag. 6).
37. A modern gold bar weighing 400 troy ounces is equivalent to about 38.5 Byzantine pounds. The initial payment to the Persians would therefore have been the equivalent of about seventy-eight modern gold bars. This is about as much gold as one could fit in a small refrigerator.
38. Hickey 2007, 302: "It would not have taken much gold to exhaust the local investment possibilities: an expenditure of 20 per cent of the estate's after-tax income (~2,600 *solidi*) on improvements would have been sufficient to build approximately 260 *sawaqi*, enough *mechanai* to irrigate over 2,000 *arourai*; i.e., about 5.5 km^2. This level of expenditure for irrigation was surely not needed annually (if in any year) on the estate." *Sawaqi* is the Arabic plural for *saqiya*, the term for the geared water-lifting device common on the Apion estate. For restrictions on munificence and lavish expenditure, see Bagnall *et al.* 1987, 10–12.
39. The rent therefore required to entice collectors to take the bid would have been unacceptably low for the imperial government.
40. Ruffini (2006) argues that the brothers' shift from the private arena to the public one was a poor business move.

Nugent describe the progression of similar situations in other historical contexts. When tax collectors could no longer carry out their duties—whether because of their own insolvency or their unwillingness—the state would take over "on an emergency basis."[41] This is precisely what occurred in Oxyrhynchus in the late first century, another period when the system of rent contracts for tax collection was in transition.[42] *P.Oxy.* 1.44, a letter from the *strategus* of the Oxyrhynchite nome to the *basilicogrammateus*, records the difficulty of finding collectors willing to take on collection contracts. The collectors claimed that they had incurred losses enough already, but the *strategus* was going to review the contracts to make the terms more favorable to the collectors. Despite apparent efforts to sweeten the deal for collectors, Jones writes, "The supply of voluntary contractors dried up, and officials were ordered to collect the tax and pay in the sum reached on the previous bid. . . . The official would have to make good the deficit out of his salary, or, more probably, charge an extra percentage on the taxpayers."[43] To resolve this problem, Azabou and Nugent explain, the state would turn to larger tax farms on longer-term contracts, which brought about "a concentration of tax farms in the hands of a few large and wealthy merchant–banker–tax farmers."[44] Such a concentration of tax collection rights is all the more likely for the Apions in Egypt, as opposed to a concentration of landownership.

Tax reforms carried out under Trajan in the late first and early second centuries and intended to remove the burden of shortfalls from the collectors point to just how this transmission of responsibility to the wealthy and prominent might occur. To relieve the difficulties facing collectors who failed to extract the amount owed from the taxpayers, the government instituted the μερισμὸς ἀνακεχωρηκότων and the μερισμὸς ἀπόρων, which divided any shortfall among the inhabitants able to pay.[45] Those wealthier inhabitants would therefore have been invested with a personal motive to ensure that their neighbors paid their taxes. The move of the wealthy people from that position, in which they bore all of the risk and reaped none of the potential benefits, to actually collecting taxes themselves (and so benefiting in some way) is not difficult to imagine. Faced with similar problems centuries later, estates like the Apions', following the trajectory described by Azabou and Nugent, filled the role the prosperous villag-

41. Azabou and Nugent 1988, 686.
42. Jones 1974, 166–68.
43. Jones 1974, 168.
44. Azabou and Nugent 1988, 686.
45. Wallace 1938, 135–46.

ers had in the earlier period but availed themselves of some of the rewards in addition to taking on the risks.

These were not changes to a different system of collection (rent to share or rent to wage) but changes in the implementation of the same rent contract system. In the example of first-century Oxyrhynchus, the rent contract system remained after collections were assumed by government officials, but the use of bids to award the collection contract had been removed. The award was given directly to an official on the same basis previously set by auction. The same is true of a transition from a situation like that of Papnouthis and Dorotheos to the Apion situation. Once a long-term rent contract had been awarded to local elites (e.g., the Apions), auctions could no longer be used to determine an appropriate level of payment expected from collectors in exchange for the right to collect. The continuity of the regions for which the Apions collected over long periods, evinced especially by the near identity of the *epoikia* collected from in *P.Oxy.* 16.1911 and 55.3804, indicates that the regions of collection were fixed once acquired.[46] Bidding at auction for shorter-term contracts would have involved changes in the areas for which the estate was collecting. It is more likely, then, that estates engaged in direct negotiation with the government for the right to collect over long periods. Coşgel and Miceli describe two mechanisms by which the payment level in such direct bargaining situations was set, depending on the volatility of the tax base: conducting frequent surveys of the tax base or using the results of a previous auction.[47] The accounts of the *pronoetai* and presumably the *apaitesima* provided such a survey of the tax base drawn up based on previous years.

Under a rent system, it makes little sense for the contracting body, here the Apion estate, to require that its collectors keep detailed records ensuring their square dealing. An advantage of the rent system is that it obviates the need for monitoring the efforts of tax collectors,[48] since the rent charged to the collectors is determined *ex ante* based on the estimated tax base. Once the representative of the state had received the amount required of Papnouthis and Dorotheos, for example, he had little need for an account of what they had actually collected.

---

46. In chapter 3, I argued that the size of a particular *prostasia* would not have changed much over time. Instead, newly added *epoikia* would have fallen into newly created *prostasiai* overseen by different *pronoetai* and would therefore have appeared in different accounts. We are simply fortunate in having *P.Oxy.* 55.3804 and 16.1911, two accounts made in different years for the same *prostasia*.
47. Coşgel and Miceli 2009, 403.
48. The state need only ensure that the collectors do not overburden the tax base with their "extracurricular" collections. See Kiser 1994, 290.

The incorporation of the private aspects of the estate into the tax collection aspects offers one explanation for the *pronoetai*'s detailed records of their collections and expenditures. But rather than a check on the honesty of the agents, the purpose of the accounts with respect to tax collection was as an aid in the estimation of the revenue base for subsequent collection years. Some estimation of the tax base was necessary, since rent systems of tax collection rely on estimates of the tax base and since the last Egyptian census occurred in the latter half of the third century.[49] If this observation is correct, responsibility for estimating the size of the tax base had fallen from the state to the estate and its collectors by the sixth century.

In other historical contexts, the size of the tax base might be measured either by the government (strictly speaking, the body contracting the collectors) or by the collectors themselves. Coşgel and Miceli argue that when collectors are the ones doing the measuring, they might "have an advantage in measuring [the tax base], owing, for example, to their local knowledge."[50] Such advantage, they continue, would be immaterial if there were a number of similarly disposed collectors vying for the right of collection, because "collectors will compete away any rents associated with their private information"; but "the collectors might be able to capture some rents if they are not sufficiently competitive."[51] Under a rent system, the combination of superior local knowledge and a lack of competition (thanks to the exclusive long-term right to collect for a given area) would have given the Apions the opportunity to extract charges in excess of the estimated tax base from the peasantry.[52] Significantly, on the lower tier, the same local knowledge advantage would have accrued to the *pronoetai* with respect to the Apions.[53] In this light, the extra 15 percent on wheat and the annual gold payment required of *pronoetai* look like the estate's effort to recoup some of the losses arising from the information imbalance.

In the first century, when the prospects for a tax farmer were not sufficiently good to attract bidders, the duty of collection fell on local officials who could compel payment from taxpayers. Their archive shows that the same problem

49. Bagnall and Frier (1994, 9–11) suggest that the census ended due to a reformation of the tax system. See also Montevecchi 1976, 77–84, for an alternate explanation of the cessation.

50. Coşgel and Miceli 2009, 407.

51. Coşgel and Miceli 2009, 407.

52. E.g., when a piece of land was more productive than assumed by the *apaitesimon*, further perquisites could be extracted.

53. Kiser (1994, 294 and n. 47) discusses the problem that large tax-farming operations responsible for determining the tax base would have in monitoring their own agents under a wage contract.

was emerging when Papnouthis and Dorotheos were operating, in the fourth century. By the sixth century, the collection lay not in the hands of government officials but in those of local elites who owned rural estates, like the Apions, playing the same role as the merchant–banker–tax farmers Azabou and Nugent describe. Kiser observes that as tax-farming operations consolidated, the state "often allowed local notables to collect a fixed amount of tax. Lump-sum negotiated payment collected by locally controlled officials or notables (usually agents of regional estates or municipalities) was common in both France and Spain, and in modified form in England, for the collection of direct taxes."[54] This trajectory of tax-farming systems recurs frequently in history and fits what we know of the Apion estate well. That the estate paid a lump sum to the state is suggested by *P.Oxy.* 1.144 (580 CE), a receipt for gold handed over by an Apion *trapezites* (estate banker) to be taken to Alexandria (though not explicitly to be handed over to the state).[55] Hardy noted that the number of *solidi* (2,160), excluding the fee for *obruza*, is equivalent to precisely 30 pounds of gold.[56] Ruffini, pointing to the three collection periods per year, argues that the text suggests "a flat fee for the Apionic estates of 90 pounds or 6,480 *solidi* for the full year," a figure "remarkably consistent" with the 6,917 *solidi* paid in taxes in *P.Oxy.* 16.1918.v from forty years earlier.[57] The round number in *P.Oxy.* 1.144 suggests that the payment made to the state—if it was indeed to the state—was a negotiated sum rather than one arising organically from collections.[58] If the trajectory Kiser describes does fit the Apion situation, the estate's upper tier operated on a rent system, paying the state a lump sum and assuming much wider tax collection responsibilities, formerly held by dispersed small-scale collectors.

The use of the rent system and lump-sum payment further explains why the Apions did not distinguish between lease collections and tax collections in their

54. Kiser 1994, 305 n. 2.
55. Zuckerman 2004, 213.
56. Hardy 1931, 56–57.
57. Ruffini 2008, 105–6. The *obruza* is not explicitly separated from the payment in *P.Oxy.* 16.1918.v, which could perhaps explain the nonround number there. *P.Oxy.* 18.2197.v, contemporary with *P.Oxy.* 1.144, has the much higher tax payment of 12,694 *solidi* from the estate, though Hickey (2008, 94–95) argues that this disparity can be explained by adaeration of grain taxes. Hickey's description of the unpublished *P.Oxy.* 18.2197.v was not available to Ruffini for his 2008 book. See also chapter 3 in the present study.
58. Transfers of gold to Constantinople are not strictly necessary for the system proposed here, since many of the state's expenditures would have been made in the same locales from which they were collected, as can be seen even at the small scale of the *pronoetes* accounts. Tax farmers have historically been crucial in this clearinghouse role, a topic discussed in greater depth in the following chapter.

accounts. Such a pooling together of rents and taxes is wholly intelligible if the estate was operating under a rent contract for the collection of taxes. Once the amount the estate would pay the government (i.e., the rent for the right to collect) had been determined, whatever they actually collected—whether from lease collections or taxes—was the estate's to keep. Wheat was separated from money, since the *embole*, the supply of grain that the state deemed it necessary to have for the residents of Constantinople and Alexandria, was handled by a different part of the imperial government.[59] This division is shown explicitly by *P.Oxy.* 1.126 (discussed in chapter 3), recording the transfer of taxation from a father to his daughter. Separating the governmental arms responsible for grain-related taxes and money taxes dates back to the Ptolemaic period, when money taxes were first introduced.[60] The special treatment of grain likely has to do with the transportation infrastructure required to move huge volumes of grain over long distances and with the political importance of supplying the staple to cities. Nevertheless, though separate from the money, the *embole* operated on a similar lump-sum system, attested by the occasional small surpluses transmuted to money by a state official and passed to the *trapezites* in the Apion *pronoetes* accounts.

While the upper tier of the Apion estate need not have had the same relationship to the imperial government as it had with the collectors who worked under it, a rent contract based on a negotiated lump sum is the most likely system governing the relationship between the state and the estate. The circumstances making this the most attractive option are quite different from those that made the rent system attractive for the relationship with the lower tier. The primary feature of the rent system that made it attractive to the imperial government was its ability to make capital available before tax collection had been carried out. This feature was also attractive to the estate, because it offered a means by which the estate could productively use what capital had been amassed. Moreover, rent systems of tax collection tend to consolidate into larger collectives like those Gascou described for the Apion administration.[61] Because the estate's payment to the government was a lump sum negotiated *ex ante*, there was no need for the estates to distinguish between their collections for rent and taxes. A rent system on the upper tier therefore answers the ques-

59. *CJ Nov.* 163 remits a year's taxes, spread over four years, but explicitly exempts wheat taxes from remission.
60. Wallace 1938, 286–92; Bingen 2007, 160–69.
61. Gascou 1985, 49–52.

tion of why the estate did not concern itself with distinguishing between rents and taxes in its accounts. Another implication is that the accounts and the *apaitesima* were intended for the estates to estimate their own tax base in order to maximize their collections relative to their lump-sum payment to the state.

A Summary of the Two Tiers Working in Concert

The tax collection system posited for the Apion estate operated on two tiers, both using rent contracts, but implemented in different ways and for different reasons. This system resulted in the Apion estate collecting more from those for whom it was responsible than it paid to the state, and this was a significant source of the estate's wealth. On the lower tier, an independent small landholder paid his fiscal obligations in kind and in billon as demanded by an Apion *pronoetes*. The *pronoetes*, pooling other such collections along with lease revenue in kind and billon, dispensed whatever wheat had been collected to the boatmen bound for Alexandria and was paid by the *embolator* for any excess above the estate's share of the *embole;* in the case of a shortfall, he would pay the *embolator* an equivalent adaerated sum. The *pronoetes* owed to the estate the amount stipulated in the *apaitesimon*, less the adjustments detailed in his account. But because collections from the smallholders and lessees were not in gold *solidi*, he engaged, like Papnouthis and Dorotheos had, in speculation to transmute billon and kind into gold. Over the course of the year, his cash obligation to the estate was paid in installments to the *trapezites*, along with whatever money the *embolator* had given him for excess wheat. Both the state and the estate benefited from using *pronoetai* under these terms, because it permitted them to deal strictly in gold for their dealings with one another, at the expense of whatever marginal profit was to be had by the *pronoetai* in gold speculation. For the estate, the risk of a poor crop, tax evasion, and failure on the speculation market was shifted to the *pronoetai*, who were contractually obligated to make up any shortfalls from the agreed-on amount and who, in turn, shifted the risk to the local peasantry by resorting to coercive measures.[62] View-

62. See *P.Oxy.* 1.136, especially lines 24–27, εἰ δὲ συμβῇ τι ἔχθεσιν γενέσθαι ἐν τοῖς προγεγραμμένοις κτήμασιν, ἐμὲ ταύτην ἀποσυμβιβάσαι τὴν δὲ ὑμῶν ὑπερφύειαν ταύτην ἑαυτῇ καταλογίσασθαι ἐν τοῖς ἐμοῖς λόγοις· τὰ δὲ ἐξωτικὰ πάντα ἐμὲ εἰς πλῆρες λημματίσαι καὶ εἰσπρᾶξαι καὶ εἰσενεγκεῖν τῷ εἰρημένῳ γεουχικῷ λόγῳ (And if any deficiency should occur on the estates aforesaid, I am to make it good and it shall be credited to your magnificence in my accounts; and I will gain and collect and pay to the aforesaid owner's account all the dues in full from the outlying properties), and lines 32–

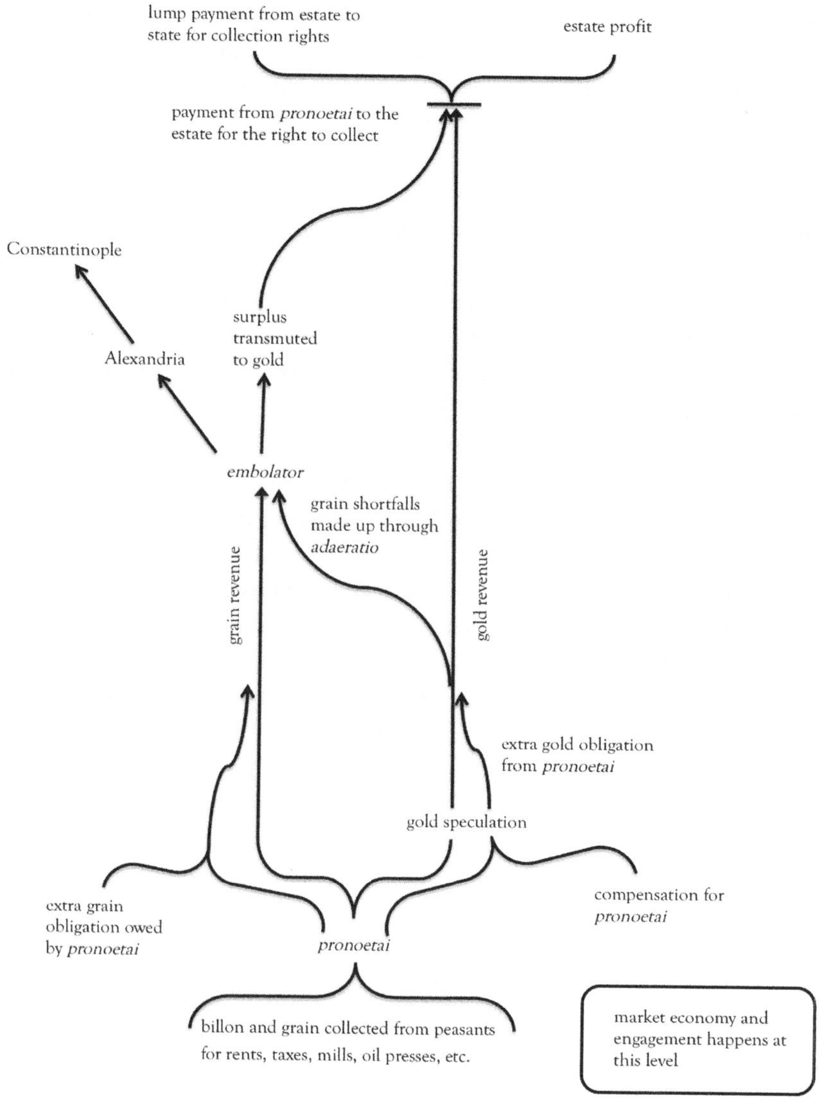

Fig. 2. The two tiers of the Apion collection apparatus working in concert

ing the Apion estate's relationship to the government as similar to that of the large-scale tax farmers who emerged in Europe many centuries later goes much of the way toward explaining how the Apion family's wealth increased in the absence of commercialized production.

Implications of a Two-Tiered Rent System

Viewing the relationship between the estate and the state as existing under a rent contract for tax collection can also answer a number of questions that have arisen in studies of the estate's role in the Egyptian economy. Clauses in labor contracts stipulating penalties for not upholding the terms,[63] wage advances treated like loans,[64] and the use of *pittakia*[65] (a type of scrip) in lieu of cash payment have all been viewed as efforts on the part of landowners to restrict the mobility of those associated with the estate.[66] Imperial legislation also restricted mobility. A number of the *Novels* of Justinian relate to the colonate and tie *coloni* to the land.[67] These efforts have usually been attributed to a scarcity of people available to work the land (whether as wage laborers or as lessees), stemming from a dip in the overall population. Banaji, however, has argued against a demographic decline in late antiquity: "It is now likely that for *most* of late antiquity population was on an upward climb and that the dominant agrarian classes were able to draw on a 'surplus' rural population."[68] The economic expansion spurred by an increase in the use of mechanical irrigation, he argues, led to greater rural prosperity and a population boom.[69] A surplus in the rural population, however, should not correlate with limitations on mobility, since such lim-

---

34, δώσω δὲ τοὺς λόγους πάσης τῆς ἐμῆς ὑποδοχῆς τοῦ τε λήμματος καὶ ἀναλώματος, καὶ τὰ ἀπὸ τῶν λογοθεσιῶν ἀποπληρώσω, εἰ λοιπαδάριος φανείην ἀκολούθως ὡς εἴρηται τοῖς ἐμοῖς ἐνταγίοις (I will render accounts of all my stewardship both of receipt and expenditure and I will make up deficiencies when the accounts are balanced the comparison of my receipts and cheques as aforesaid shows me to be in arrears). The translations here are the editor's.

63. Banaji 2001, 190–91.
64. Banaji 2001, 203–5. The harsh terms in many of these contracts would have essentially indentured debtors to their creditors. The concept is known as "debt bondage." The possibility of detention of family members in estate prisons would have mitigated the risk of flight.
65. Sarris 2006, 92–93.
66. "Those associated with the estates" are lessees and people paying taxes through the estate, but under Banaji's formulation, they are wage laborers. See Kehoe 2003, 716–17.
67. Banaji 2001, 207–11.
68. Banaji 2001, 215; emphasis in original.
69. Banaji 2001, 206–7, 214–15.

itations are meant to counteract the unfavorable pressures on landowners that can result from high demand for a small supply of workers and tenants.[70]

In an attempt to reconcile the apparently conflicting phenomena of a surplus rural population and efforts to restrict its mobility, Banaji argues that the legislation aimed at restricting worker mobility was not connected with labor supply but, rather, facilitated the state's efforts at tracking the "taxable labour capacity of estates," so that "landowners were thus required to maintain a list of all regular labourers who counted for taxation purposes."[71] Like Banaji, Sarris sees evidence of population growth in late antiquity. For evidence of growth, he relies on Ward-Perkins' survey of "the archaeology," which argues that the eastern empire reached peak population and population density in the fifth and sixth centuries.

On Egypt's population specifically, however, Ward-Perkins relies not on archaeology but on the papyrological evidence for greater use of mechanical irrigation, indicating greater exploitation of marginal land, a phenomenon associated with increased population density on the limestone massifs in Syria.[72] But artificial irrigation was used in Egypt not only to make marginal land more productive but to grow crops requiring perennial irrigation or to have more than one harvest per year on a single plot of land.[73] The use of artificial irrigation does not necessarily indicate that there was population growth in Egypt. Moreover, population growth in one place does not necessarily entail growth everywhere; as Kehoe writes, "for urban areas, Late Roman Egypt presents a varied picture, with some cities apparently maintaining prosperity and others declining."[74] The same is surely true when comparing Egypt to the even more geographically and economically disparate locales that Ward-Perkins surveys.

Kehoe notes further that imperial legislation was not restricted to Egypt and would have applied elsewhere in the empire, including places that calculated taxation differently from Egypt.[75] He argues that legislation concerned with the mobility of *georgoi* was indeed connected with the labor supply and

70. Brass 2005, 142–43 n. 48. In such a situation, one estate might offer higher wages or more favorable leases and attract labor away from another.

71. Banaji 2001, 211. The activity Banaji describes might be estimating the tax base, an activity that I argue had fallen to the estate by the time of the Apions.

72. Ward-Perkins 2000, 321.

73. Gardens and vineyards required constant year-round irrigation. Fayyum evidence points to many different crops on artificially irrigated land: see Johnson and West 1949, 11–15.

74. Kehoe 2003, 718 n. 22.

75. Kehoe 2003, 717.

stemmed from the imperial government's desire that estates retain sufficient labor to remain productive, regardless of how taxes were calculated.[76] Kehoe thus sees the conflict in Banaji's argument as insoluble and claims that there was instead a population shortfall: "In Egypt it seems likely that the population reached its peak in the 2nd c, and, after a decline in the 3rd c, regained some ground in the next two centuries."[77] This shortfall, Kehoe argues, drove the efforts at the imperial and estate levels to restrict the mobility.

In light of this varied picture, Sarris' and Ward-Perkins' arguments for population growth are less secure, but Kehoe's objection to Banaji is also problematic. If trends in population and prosperity differed from location to location, imperial legislation might have been crafted to address needs and problems arising in some (or many) parts of the empire but not in others. It is conceivable that the laws restricting mobility were made with Egypt and its basis of taxation in mind and had little practical application where the basis was different.[78] Therefore, Banaji's argument cannot be disregarded only on the grounds Kehoe offers.

Even if it is granted that population numbers increased in Egypt in late antiquity, population growth (size relative to previous population) does not necessarily entail a population surplus (size relative to the demand for people to work the land). In other words, there may have been growth insufficient to exceed labor demands. This observation vitiates Banaji's underlying assumption that an increase in overall population means an increase in the population of lessees and workers. Banaji also neglects to consider another possibility, that the increase in Egypt's population was in the number of small landholders or craftsmen, without an increase in the number of available lessees and workers.[79] Landowners might have desired to restrict mobility even when the overall rural population had risen, since demand from smaller landowners for a relatively scarce supply of casual labor would be greater. Banaji's explanation also falters in explaining the private efforts of the estates to restrict mobility. He argues that these efforts stemmed from "the high instability of labor, with workers frequently deserting jobs."[80] But this explanation merely pushes the question

76. Kehoe 2003, 717.
77. Kehoe 2003, 718 n. 22.
78. There are other instances in which imperial legislation was only applied to one province: e.g., *CJ* 1.40 applied (initially) only to Italy; *CJ Nov.* 154 concerns unlawful marriage in Mesopotamia; and *CJ Nov.* 145 concerns only certain cities in Asia Minor.
79. As Brass (2005, 141 n. 38) puts it, "Banaji is making an assumption that equates population growth simply with an over-supply of workers, without asking into what other occupational channels . . . such expansion might be diverted."
80. Banaji 2001, 205.

back a step to why labor was unstable, and the answer to this question militates against Banaji's claims of surplus labor: "If workers were much sought-after, and higher wages consequently on offer elsewhere, then this would account both for their 'reluctance' to remain with a single employer (= at a given wage rate) and for the countervailing need of landowners generally to combine the decasualization of employment with the use of coercive mechanisms."[81]

Efforts to restrict the mobility of those working the land in late antique Oxyrhynchus might have occurred in four possible situations: (1) there was population growth, but efforts to restrict movement were related to tracking the taxable capacity of estates, not to the supply of labor (Banaji); (2) there was not population growth, and therefore a scarcity of labor obtained, so the state and the estates both desired to restrict the mobility of labor (Kehoe); (3) there was population growth but not in excess of the demand for labor, so labor was scarce; or (4) there was population growth but not among those from whom labor was demanded, so labor was scarce. Determining which of these four situations was actually the case in Egypt by focusing on population demands the extremely difficult task of local demographic analysis. The rent model of tax collection proposed here sidesteps this thorny issue and can explain restrictions on the mobility of labor both on the part of estates and on the part of the imperial government, irrespective of population.

Restricting the mobility of those who work the land also has the effect of stabilizing the returns expected from each unit of taxation, at the expense of maximal efficiency; that is, it is a purchase of low variance.[82] If there were population shortfalls, even restricted to certain areas, then blanket legislation would have solved the problem in those areas and had little or no impact where the population level sufficed to maintain productive land. The appeal of stable, predictable returns can explain why the imperial government would choose to impose restrictions on mobility. As for the private efforts, maintaining the number of people whose taxes fell under the Apion umbrella would have increased the scale of their tax-farming operation. The more land for which they were fiscally responsible and that was being productively worked, regardless of tenure, the more the estate stood to gain from tax farming. In the model pro-

81. Brass 2005, 128

82. The maximally efficient distribution of workers to land would occur in the absence of restrictions on mobility. E.g., if piece of land *x* is potentially highly productive but short on labor, restricting the mobility of workers on neighboring, less productive piece of land *y* reduces overall efficiency. The upside is that the state restricting mobility knows the taxes it can expect from *x* and *y*, even though the units as a whole produce less than they would without mobility restrictions.

posed here, bringing land and small landowners under the estate's taxation umbrella was a means for the estate to increase its share of the tax collection burden, which, in turn, increased the absolute amount it could make from its tax collection efforts. If the expenditure necessary to collect more taxes was less than the amount it stood to gain, expansion of the umbrella was a moneymaking proposition. Once the collection infrastructure was in place, economies of scale suggest that the condition would have been satisfied.

Hence, even in a period with a labor surplus, landowners might have opportunistically taken advantage of legislation restricting mobility and made efforts of their own to prevent lessees and workers from leaving, thereby sustaining the size of their tax umbrella. Another impetus for the efforts to restrict mobility was the economic pressure placed on lessees by collection practices. If the burdens placed on them became severe, flight might have been an attractive option. The desire to restrict mobility could therefore still arise even in a period with a rural surplus population, if that population was sufficiently pressed.

The use of a rent system can also explain the prevalence of mechanical irrigation on the Apion estate, since it could augment the total area on which taxes were due. An estate owning land made newly productive by an irrigation machine would have to pay the tax on that land, but the machines could bring in revenue as well by providing water to neighboring land without direct access to floodwaters or an irrigator of its own. Evidence for this practice exists from the advent of widespread use of *mechanai*, water-lifting machines. *P.Ross.Georg.* 2.19, a lease from 141 CE, permits the lessee to sell water rights to neighbors. Evidence that this practice continued at least into the sixth century comes from several leases of ἄνυδρος land—land relying on an irrigation machine installed on a different piece of land.[83] Most of these leases are from sixth-century Aphrodito, with none extant from sixth-century Oxyrhynchus. But, as discussed in chapter 2, this absence is likely due to the waning importance of lease documents there, not the absence of leasing itself. Such agreements would have been lucrative for the Apion estate in two ways: from selling the rights to the water (or charging correspondingly higher lease rates, as the case may be) and from increasing the land available to smaller landholders. These smaller landholders would have been entirely dependent on the estate for their livelihoods and would also have been subject to its tax collection efforts.

The gross cash *lemmata* (target receipts) of the Apion estate increased

83. E.g., *P.Lond.* 5.1689, 1693, 1770.

roughly twofold between the years recorded by *P.Oxy.* 16.1918.v and 18.2196.v.[84] At the end of chapter 3, I argued that this increase came about not from increases in either taxes or production but chiefly from increases in the amount of land either owned by the Apions or for which they collected taxes. It has been a matter of some debate whether the estates can be seen as expanding or merely taking responsibility for tax collection from greater numbers of smallholders. The difficulty stems again from the lack of concern for distinguishing between rents and taxes in the extant accounts of the Apion estate. But the evident lack of concern reflects the insignificance of the distinction for the estate: the taxes and perquisites gotten by Apion collectors from smallholders and lessees alike extracted a great deal of any surplus beyond the cultivators' bare subsistence level, irrespective of land tenure. Even in cases where lessees might seem more prosperous, owning their own land, the estate could become involved. Chapter 14 of Justinian's *Novel* 128 stipulates that a landowner was not obliged to pay taxes on the lands owned by those *coloni* responsible to him,[85] unless he willingly made himself so liable.[86] This was clearly the situation for the Isaac son of Melas in *P.Oxy.* 55.3804.92, who made a payment to an Apion *pronoetes* for ἰδίας γῆς, private land. This legislation was highly favorable to large estate owners like the Apions, since it permitted them to assume liability for the taxes on a piece of land on their own terms, that is, when it was financially beneficial for them to do so.

Another area of disagreement in examinations of the estates of Byzantine Egypt is whether the relationship between influential landholders and the state was cooperative or antagonistic. Sarris has described the recent trend in scholarship "to emphasise co-operation between public and private authority, aristocrat and emperor."[87] Indeed, Gascou's model of fiscal shares implies a close relationship between the public and private spheres. Pushing back against this idea, Sarris sees the relationship as "a bitter struggle between the person of the

84. Hickey 2008, 99.
85. These would be *coloni* leasing the landowner's land. A *colonus* might rent some portion of the land he works and own some other portion. Banaji interprets *coloni adscripticii* / *georgoi enapographoi* idiosyncratically as primarily wage laborers. For criticism of this view, see Brass 2005.
86. Μηδεὶς δὲ τὸ σύνολον ἐνοχλείσθω ὑπὲρ συνελείας γηδίων ἅπερ οὐ κέκτηται ἀλλὰ καὶ εἰ συμβαίη γεωργούς τινι προσήκοντας ἢ ἐναπογράφους ἰδίαν ἔχειν κτῆσιν, ἐκείνους ὑπὲρ αὐτῆς τὰς δημοσίας εἰσπράττεσθαι συντλείας, τοῦ δεσπότου αὐτῶν μηδεμίαν ὄχλησιν ὑπὲρ αὐτῶν ὑπομένοντος, εἰ μὴ ὡς εἰκὸς αὐτὸς ἰδίᾳ προαιρέσει τῇ τοιαύτῃ συντελείᾳ ἑαυτὸν ἐποίησεν ἔνοχον. Again, the assumption that an estate owner would not do something for nothing implies that if this obligation was taken on willingly, he must have stood to gain from it in certain circumstances.
87. Sarris 2006, 149.

emperor and elements within the political and social elite of the empire."[88] But to describe the relationship between aristocratic estate owners like the Apions as either cooperative or antagonistic is to miscategorize it. If the state and the estate were involved in a rent contract for the collection of taxes, it is better to view the state and the estate as parties in a negotiation, each advocating for its best interest in a mutually beneficial arrangement. This view entails certain actions appearing antagonistic but ending in a mutually beneficial, cooperative agreement, a feature that holds for any negotiated settlement, whether between a buyer and seller, political parties, or unions and management. As evidence of a bitter struggle, Sarris offers the example of Justinian's *Edict* 13, which chides those involved with the collection of taxes, including imperial officeholders, for their skimming of collections from Egypt.[89] Yet the public statements of the emperor disassociating himself from widely hated tax collectors were clearly propagandistic (a point that Sarris himself admits)[90] but also gained him negotiating leverage by stoking that hatred and casting himself as the defender of the people from the tax collectors. The tactic diverted blame for onerous taxes from the emperor, while still granting the emperor the ability to garner goodwill from occasional tax remissions (which might not relieve collectors of their own obligations to the state).[91]

Conclusion

The Apion estate was engaged in the collection of taxes for cultivators in its area. Whether these cultivators were lessees or smaller independent holders does not particularly matter, since the taxes collected went into the same pool as what was collected from leases; from that larger pool, the Apions paid the taxes on their own land and that of the smaller landholders according to the contract negotiated with the state. Collections were accomplished using two tiers, each operating on a rent system wherein a fixed amount was handed over to the contracting party and wherein collections above that fixed amount were compensation for collection. On the upper tier, the contracting party was the

88. Sarris 2006, 3.
89. Sarris 2006, 2–3.
90. Sarris 2006, 3.
91. E.g., *CJ Nov.* 163 demands that any collections already made on remitted taxes must be handed over to the state.

state; on the lower tier, it was the estate. The documents in the Apion dossier suggest that collections on the lower tier were subcontracted to *pronoetai* and other agents of the estate under a rent system, and circumstances in force at the lower tier—a preexisting accounting system and the difficulty of making collections in kind—support that conclusion. A rent system of collection requires an estimate of the tax base, and the *apaitesima* and *pronoetes* accounts look to be attempts on the part of the estate to get just that. The upper tier of the estate's collection apparatus also operated under a rent system, contracted by the state, though for different reasons from those on the lower tier. The system was primarily attractive to the state because it made capital available for its exigent expenditures. As needs for capital increased, the collection often consolidated into the hands of larger, more prominent collectors. The system was also valuable for the estate because it was one of few ways in which it could productively put accumulated wealth to use.

A number of historical examples parallel the transition from the rent system apparent in the Papnouthis and Dorotheos archive to the one posited for the Apion estate. When social and economic factors made it unattractive for collectors to assume the risk of the contract, the problem was often solved by granting longer-term collection contracts to larger collectors. This tendency to place collection into the hands of the wealthy can be explained by looking at second-century legislation that was aimed at a similar problem and that transferred much of the risk for shortfalls onto the most prominent taxpayers, making the elites keenly interested in ensuring that their neighbors of lesser means paid their taxes.

The consolidation of collection also changed the terms of the rent contracts with the state. Granting the estate exclusive collection rights for a long period had the effect of making the estate, rather than the state (as was the case for Papnouthis and Dorotheos), responsible for the estimation of the tax base. The disparity in local knowledge between the estate and the state could be exploited by the estate for its own gain. But the estate's own use of *pronoetai* to estimate the tax base left them facing the same type of knowledge disparity. To counter it, estate owners imposed fees on the perquisites that their collectors extracted.

There is evidence that the estate's upper tier paid the state a round, lump sum annually. This fits into historical patterns in which tax collection through rent contracts consolidated into the hands of local elites. Such lump-sum payments on the upper tier can further explain why the accounts of the Apion estate are not at pains to distinguish between rent collections and tax collections:

the lump payment would be drawn from the larger pool of total collections, with the remainder left to estate coffers.

The picture of tax collection by the Apion estate offered here can address some of the vexing issues scholars have been grappling with while studying the role of the estate in the economy of Byzantine Egypt. The efforts on the part of the state and estates to restrict the mobility of those who cultivated the land do not accord with claims of a surplus population in late antique Egypt. The use of rent contracts for tax collection on the Apion estate can account for efforts to restrict mobility irrespective of population: the more people the estate collected from, the greater their revenue from tax collection would be. In addition, the significant burden the estate's collection practices placed on cultivators made the option of flight attractive, even if there was a population surplus. Expansion of mechanical irrigation was linked to the rent system of tax collection, since more arable or more highly productive land would have meant more taxes to be collected by the Apions. The question of whether estate revenues increased in the sixth century because of expansion of ownership or expansion of collections also takes on a different character: land owned by the estate did not produce a marketable surplus, and land that the estate owned and leased and the land it did not own but for which it collected taxes, both contributed to earnings from tax collection. The question of land tenure as it relates to estate receipts therefore becomes immaterial. Finally, characterizing the state and the estate as either cooperative or antagonistic fails to recognize that both were parties in a negotiation, each lobbying for its own interest in arriving at a mutually beneficial arrangement.

CHAPTER 5

Analogues to Apion Tax Farming

The *pronoetes* accounts indicate that the Apion estate's lower tier of administration used a rent system for the collection of taxes on its own land and that of its neighbors. In chapter 4, I argued that the forms that the relationship between the state and the estate's upper tier could take were fairly circumscribed, and the evidence, though fragmentary, pointed to a rent system. This chapter presents the emergence of tax-farming systems (a subset of the rent system) in Athens, Ptolemaic Egypt, and republican Rome as historical analogues for the development of the Apion tax collection system out of the system apparent in the Papnouthis and Dorotheos archive. These examples are offered as evidence that the model constructed in the foregoing chapters is not eccentric but with precedent and that it reflects often natural developments of tax-farming systems. They are also offered as analogues that allow inferences about the Apion estate and Byzantine Egypt that cannot be directly observed from contemporary evidence. The chapter then presents France's tax collection system from the Middle Ages through the seventeenth century as an analogue for the development of a two-tiered system in a context similar to that of the Apion estate. Examining the motivations for and ramifications of the development of the French system offers interpretive possibilities for the Apion system and the estate's place in Byzantine Egypt.[1] More generally, the similarities between the Apion collection system and other, more fully understood historical instances of tax farming can help to fill in gaps in our understanding of estates in Byzantine Egypt.

1. This discussion of the background on analogous examples is not meant to provide detailed accounts of those very broad, complex, and bibliographically imposing subjects. The focus here is on the specific ways in which they explicate the Apion situation.

Consolidation and the Formation of Collection Syndicates

Athens

The system of tax farming employed by the Athenians conforms to the tendency noted by Kiser for distributed, small-scale collectors to consolidate into larger syndicates revolving around a wealthy elite.[2] While liturgies predominated, a variety of taxes still played a role in financing Athens. Most taxes collected by the city were indirect; that is, the state collected not from the people liable to the tax but from intermediaries who took payment on transactions.[3] Such indirect taxes included the import and export tax (πεντηκοστή), the harbor tax (ἐλλιμένιον), and the tax on prostitutes (πορνικόν). Aristotle's *Athenaion politeia* prescribes that the right to collect these taxes should be sold to the highest bidder. In other words, they were to be farmed.[4] The highest bidder was to pay half of the bid, the προκαταβολή, up front and the other half, the προσκατάβλημα, after six months.[5] An individual collector could bid on a single minor tax or on several small taxes that had been bundled together and sold as a lot.[6] Collectors were not always of significant means, so a surety was required of them to guarantee payment.[7] For taxes that generated high revenues, such as the πεντηκοστή, or for large bundles of smaller taxes, even a wealthy person might have had difficulty covering the bid on his own.[8] For these major taxes, associations of wealthy individuals would take out shares in the farming contract bid on by a head tax farmer, the τελωνάρχης.[9] Andocides describes breaking up one such association that was colluding to keep the price of the bid

---

2. Mokyr 2007, s.v. "tax farming."
3. A modern example of an indirect tax is a sales tax, with the merchant acting as the intermediary from whom the state collects the tax, as opposed to the customer who bears the burden of payment. In other words, the person paying an indirect tax to the state can pass the cost on to someone else, whereas the person paying a direct tax (e.g., income tax) cannot. A rent model for such taxes accords well with Coşgel and Miceli's model, since the high costs of monitoring myriad small transactions would have made the simpler prospect of renting out collections for a fixed sum highly attractive.
4. Jones 1974, 153 and n. 18; *Ath. pol.* 47.
5. Youtie 1967, 9.
6. Andreades 1933, 160.
7. Plutarch (*Alc.* 5) relates an anecdote in which Alcibiades acts as surety for a *metic* whom he has compelled to outbid the other tax farmers.
8. Jones 1974, 153 and n. 10: revenue from this tax attested as high as two hundred talents annually, and shares were still taken out for the "exceptionally low" yield of thirty talents attested in Andocides *De myst.* 133.
9. Andreades 1933, 160 n. 8.

down,[10] and Lycurgus mentions that Leocrates had a share in the farming of the πεντηκοστή.[11] In summary, indirect taxes in Athens were bundled together into substantial sums, and the contracts for them were assumed by groups of wealthy citizens.

The special case of the direct tax in Athens is of particular interest in comparison with the model proposed for the Apion estate. The εἰσφορά, "a special tax on capital intended to cover an urgent national need,"[12] was likely first implemented in 428/7, during the Peloponnesian War.[13] The precise nature of the εἰσφορά in its initial formulation has been a matter of some dispute,[14] but the tax appears to have been a determined sum divided evenly among the wealthiest citizens of Athens and collected directly under the authority of the generals.[15] After 378/7, the εἰσφορά underwent a series of reforms that made the tax a regular part of revenue collection by the Athenian state, rather than the emergency measure it had been before. The method of collection effected by these changes parallel, on a smaller scale, the tendencies observed in Byzantine Egypt by Gascou, in which the Apion family acted as part of a syndicate of local elites collecting taxes on behalf of their neighbors and paying the state.[16] Similarly, in Athens, the εἰσφορά was not collected directly from the fifteen hundred or so people liable to the tax;[17] rather, one hundred groups (συμμορίαι) liable for the same amount of the tax were formed. Each συμμορία was headed by its three richest members, who paid the προεισφορά, an up-front payment of the whole amount due from their συμμορία. It was then left to the three hundred leading members to recoup this amount (less their own contributions) from the other members of the συμμορίαι, in whatever manner they could. As Gascou describes the Apion estate, groups comprising a wealthy subset of those liable to the tax paid the state the amount of the tax on behalf of everyone liable to the tax. Similarly, both direct and indirect tax collection in Athens came to be carried out through wealthy syndicates. Collection of the direct εἰσφορά was con-

---

10. *De myst.* 1.133.
11. *In Leocratem* 19.
12. Andreades 1933, 327. On the εἰσφορά, see Ste. Croix 1953; Christ 2007.
13. According to Thucydides 3.19, this was the first time the Athenians exacted the εἰσφορά, but it is unclear exactly what the word πρῶτον indicates in the context (whether absolutely, since the start of the war, since the start of his history, or so on). There is some evidence that the tax dates back to Solon. See Christ 2007, 54–55; Thomsen 1964, 14–23; Andreades 1933, 330–34.
14. See Christ 2007 for the terms of the debate.
15. Christ 2007, 59–60.
16. Gascou 1985, especially 49–52. See also chapter 1, n. 27.
17. Christ 2007, 63.

solidated by design, while consolidated collection of the indirect taxes arose from necessity. As was the case on the Apion estate, collecting both direct and indirect taxes in Athens entailed partial or entire payment to the *polis* in anticipation of collection.

Jones singles out the εἰσφορά as one Athenian tax that was not farmed.[18] This is true in the narrow sense that the tax was not collected by the class of τελῶναι (tax farmers). But from a systematic point of view, the collections were carried out on a rent model. Through the use of the συμμορίαι and the τίμημα (a valuation of the property to be taxed), the Athenians were at pains to measure and standardize the tax base.[19] This type of measurement activity correlates with a rent system on Coşgel and Miceli's model. There is no evidence that the three hundred members providing the advance were remunerated in cash for their collection efforts, but this is not integral to the rent system of collection. In other milieus, collectors might be compensated in nonmonetary ways, such as by exemption from military service.[20] One clear benefit to the three hundred was avoiding the opprobrium of the other citizens for perceived stinginess in their acts of civic giving, a perception potentially disastrous in litigious Athens. Payment or nonpayment of the εἰσφορά was used as ammunition in the Athenian law courts.[21] Moreover, the likely purpose of the reform to the εἰσφορά and its certain result were to expedite access to the tax by having wealthy citizens, able to bear the cash-flow demands, advance the sum, in the form of the προεισφορά, in anticipation of actual collection. Both the explicitly farmed indirect taxes and the direct εἰσφορά, which was also collected on a rent system, display the tendency of these systems to consolidate from dispersed independent collectors into syndicates headed by those with the greatest wealth and social capital.

Athens demonstrates the role that the possession of capital played in reaping benefits from tax farming, especially in the shares taken out for the farming of indirect taxes. The benefits derived from collecting indirect taxes self-reinforce: the wealthy who were able to take on the tax collection responsibility

---

18. Jones 1974, 154.
19. Andreades 1979, 334–37.
20. The *publicani* were granted exemption from military service as compensation in exceptional circumstances during the fighting against Hannibal in 215 BC (Badian 1983, 16–17). Other arrangements have also been observed: in Moghul India, military and civil officers were compensated for their services with tax collection rights (Habib 1963, especially 259–73).
21. Lysias (19.42–43, 21.1–5) uses the payment of *eisphora* and other liturgies as a defense. Isaeus (5.45) reproaches someone for his stinginess in his liturgies. See Andreades 1933, 132 and n. 2, 358–61.

became more wealthy and therefore able to take on more and larger collection responsibilities, with the potential of still greater benefit. Even in the case of the εἰσφορά, where a profit motive was absent, the collection responsibilities concentrated into the hands of a wealthy elite. The trajectory of tax collection in Byzantine Egypt from the fourth to the sixth centuries was similarly determined. The conditions attendant to the Apions' rising status—a state in need of funds, small-scale collectors unable to advance those funds, and locally prominent estate owners with a collection apparatus and special relationships with the imperial government—permitted the Apion family to assume tax collection responsibilities that were once the purview of many independent collectors and to rise in wealth due to the self-reinforcing benefits of tax farming reaped by the already relatively affluent.

The *Publicani*

The *publicani* were the tax collectors of the Roman Republic and were "an integral part of the *res publica* as far back as we can observe it or trace it."[22] Along with collecting taxes, the *publicani* were involved in other activities with a public bent, such as building and road construction, mining operations, and requisitioning goods for the army. The *publicani* were therefore responsible for collections from the public or from public properties (e.g., mines) and for expenditures on the public's behalf.[23] In the former capacity, they handed money to the state for the right to collect from the public; in the latter, they took money from the state to perform a service for the public. For the expenditures, they were required to provide collateral, in case they failed to complete a project; and for the collections, they were required to pay all or part of the bid up front. Consequently, both roles required the *publicani* to possess a certain level of capital. Early on, the *publicani* banded together in their various undertakings, to form *societates*.[24] Badian argues that the purpose of these groups was to distribute risk, since bidding on the contracts required large amounts of collateral and sureties.[25] On this view, the growth of the *societates* and other tax-farming syndicates operated on the same principle as insurance companies: small returns

22. Badian 1983, 16.
23. Levi 1988, 86.
24. Badian 1983, 67–82; Youtie 1967, 10. These groups eventually were legally incorporated, becoming perhaps the first examples of the modern concept of corporate personhood.
25. Badian 1983, 69.

from a large number of bets more than offset occasional large losses on a minority of them. The greater the number and the variety of the bets were, the more sizable the offset was.[26] As was the case for the Athenian τελῶναι, the sheer cost of many undertakings—beyond the capacity of any single person to finance—also likely spurred the consolidation of the *publicani* into *societates*.[27] The collection of taxes required the same risk mitigation and cost distribution as expenditure projects, demanding capital up front and entailing a great deal of risk.

The archive of Papnouthis and Dorotheos shows that small-scale collectors in fourth-century Egypt faced the same basic difficulties in bidding on tax rights as the early *publicani*: acquiring sufficient capital to pay the bid and assuming the risk of being unable to collect the taxes. The solutions that the *publicani* employed to address these problems can be found in the collection system of the Apion estate. In chapter 3, it was argued that the relatively low social status of collectors like Papnouthis and Dorotheos increased the risks they assumed, because it exposed them to exploitation by those above and below them in the social hierarchy, while higher-status collectors, like the Apions, were immune to these difficulties. Badian's explanation for the consolidation of the *publicani* makes better sense of why those on a higher social stratum, like the Apions, would be more suited to dealing with the risks than were Papnouthis and Dorotheos. The *publicani* banded together to increase the pool of bets and distribute the risk. The size of the Apions' holdings had much the same effect, and their involvement in the groups of collectors would have likewise dispersed the risk they were assuming.[28] Moreover, whereas a small-scale collector might bid on the rights to a single village, the scattered geographical layout of Apion holdings distributed many of the risks to collection, such as local flooding and the breaching of dikes. As large landholders, the Apions were also able to collect taxes from those over whom they already had some control in their role as landlord or those who depended on the Apion *mechanai* for access to water.

---

26. Groups of *publicani* eventually grew so large and influential that they could operate as cartels, dictating the price of the bids to the state. See Badian 1983, 74.
27. Badian (1983, 67–68) notes that the richest man in Rome in the time of Cicero and Caesar was said to have had a fortune of forty-eight million *denarii* and that a building project one hundred years earlier was contracted at forty-five million *denarii*. That amount, he notes, was also 450 times the property requirement for the equestrian class, to which most *publicani* belonged.
28. The largest contributor in a group, like the Apions, would have assumed some of the risk otherwise born by the smaller members, but such relationships remained reciprocal as long as the smaller members together held a significant amount of land. Indeed, in the 560s, the Apions were predominant in Oxyrhynchus but were not the only significant landholders. See Hickey 2008, 297, fig. 14.3, for a distribution of shares among landholders.

While the surviving Apion leases mostly indicate that the lessor was responsible for the taxes owed on the land, the amount of tax owed by the Apions on a particular piece of land would have been included in the determination of the lease price, making the tenant responsible for the taxes *de facto*.[29] As a result, the situation is akin to an indirect tax: while the Apions were responsible to the state for the tax, they were not the party ultimately bearing its burden, just as those collecting harbor dues in Athens paid the state while others bore the burden. The taxes over which the Apions had collection rights would not have been separated from the other revenue to which they were entitled—indeed, they were not separated in the *pronoetai* accounts. Because the Apions were leasing and collecting revenue separate from taxes, the collection apparatus was already in place and largely the same as a tax collection apparatus.

Another notable similarity between the *publicani* and the Apions is the involvement of private entities in public financing. The *publicani* were involved in loaning the Asian cities huge sums to pay off the indemnities Sulla imposed on them in 84 BCE. When the cities were unable to pay the *publicani*, they were forced to accept their loans on unfavorable terms. Predictably, this placed the cities in perpetual debt to the *publicani*.[30] Money lending was among the varied roles that tax farmers played in the financial workings of both local and empire-wide government. The possibilities for credit that tax-farming systems create are a crucial part of their use and can explain both why tax farming was used and why it persisted despite any drawbacks. The extent to which the Apions were involved in the credit aspects of tax farming is further discussed later in this chapter, in connection with the more fully understood French tax-farming system. One conclusion to be drawn at this point with respect to the Apion estate in Byzantine Egypt is how absolutely normal it was in the ancient world for private entities to be insinuated into the financial workings of the state. To expect a division in estate accounts between public and private finances is an anachronism.

Operating on Many Tiers

The example of the *publicani* also offers substantial evidence of subcontracted local employees making collections. Youtie notes that the rendering of the Greek

29. *P.Flor.* 3.325; *P.Oxy.* 63.4390. See also *P.Oxy.* 6.913 (not from Apion, but from fifth-century Oxyrhynchus).
30. Jones 1974, 118–21.

τελῶναι into *publicani* in the Latin New Testament misunderstands both terms, not least because it conflates several layers of the collection hierarchy.[31] The reviled so-called *publicani* grouped rhetorically with prostitutes and sinners were actually local collectors employed by or collaborating with the *publicani*.[32] Youtie writes, "The Roman publican, a knight and a member of a *societas publicanorum*, powerful in wealth and influence, would have blushed with shame at this lowly use of his professional title."[33] The large collection operations of the *publicani* functioned on several tiers, as must have all large collection operations in the premodern world. The difficulty of communication and transport made direct involvement logistically unmanageable, and the status of those at the higher echelons of collection operations made it socially unthinkable. Bagnall writes of the liturgists of fourth-century Egypt, "It is impossible to imagine the members of the top 100 families of Oxyrhynchos or Hermopolis, who held most city liturgies connected with taxes and would have to pay up if they were not delivered in full to the imperial government, going about the dusty countryside collecting a few artabas here, a few grains of gold there, from their social inferiors."[34] The same sentiment applies to those contracting with the state to make tax collections over large areas, be they the *publicani* or the Apions.

A multitiered collection system becomes particularly apparent when the *publicani* were permitted to bid on the lucrative tithes due from Asia. The *publicani* with the winning bid would negotiate with the Asian cities for the payment of a lump sum. The cities must have used some collection system of their own to obtain these payments, implying a tier below the *publicani*, about which the *publicani* likely cared little as long as the cities made their payments. Even in Athens, where the collection system for the εἰσφορά was not particularly large, the efforts used several tiers. The three hundred responsible for the προεισφορά existed on an upper tier, interacting with the *polis*. The three hundred, in turn, must have had some means of recouping those funds from the other members of their συμμορία. Social forces again make it very difficult to envision the three hundred wealthiest people in Athens making the collections themselves. While the methods employed on the lower tier are obscure, that some lower collection tier was in place is clear.

---

31. Youtie 1967, 8. The *publicani* appear in the New Testament at *Mark* 2.16, *Matthew* 9.10–11, and *Luke* 5.30 and 19.2.
32. Badian 1983, 11.
33. Youtie 1967, 8.
34. Bagnall 1993, 158.

In each of these examples, those who were contracted to collect taxes on a large scale were faced with the same problem as the states that had hired them, and they had at hand the same solutions: rent, wage, and share systems. Difficulties in communication and transportation in the premodern world made multitiered, delegation-dependent operations essential to large-scale collection systems. For the contractors physically to make collections from all those who owed them was simply impractical. The type of collection system used by the Apions therefore required multiple tiers. Where close monitoring of geographically distributed collectors or the central *post facto* counting of all collections was prohibitively expensive or where the possibilities of speculation and tax anticipation were attractive, the rent model arose on the lower tiers. On the Apion estate, the two-tiered collection system was large in scale and widely distributed, and speculation was used to convert collections in billon and kind into gold. The use of a rent system on the lower tier, therefore, would have shifted risk and also allowed the upper tier (the estate) to derive some benefit from the speculation through contractual arrangements.

Speculation and Tax Farming

Given that Apion *pronoetai* made collections in kind and billon but payments to the estate in gold, the lower-tier Apion agents likely engaged in the same type of speculation as Papnouthis and Dorotheos. The collections made by the *pronoetai* on grant from the Apions were effectively a loan of capital from the estate, offering potential for making money through speculation with earnings exceeding the interest due on the loan. This course is all the more likely in light of the fact that the *pronoetai* were obliged to hand over a substantial portion of the perquisites that they extracted from the lessees and taxpayers and that functioned as interest on the loan of the principal.[35] Parallels for speculation that used collections as principal exist elsewhere where tax farming on multiple tiers was employed. For example, Webber and Wildavsky note that collectors in Rome in the first century BCE would accept payment in kind from cultivators, offering a very low price, when the collectors knew that urban markets would bear a much higher price.[36] Handing over to the state the original value owed in

35. In the extant examples, the *pronoetai* handed over around 15 percent on grain collection and 12 or more *solidi* per year. See chapter 3.

36. Webber and Wildavsky 1986, 117–18. See also Frank 1962, 154.

money, the collectors were able to keep the remainder. In this way, the Roman collectors speculated on the grain market by using their knowledge of markets inaccessible to the cultivators from whom they collected. Webber and Wildavsky write, "The principal opportunity for extra gain stemmed from the absence of a market mechanism for converting agricultural produce into money. As a barter economy still existed in the agricultural districts, local subcontractors profited by converting taxes paid in grain into the money payments demanded by the Roman Senate."[37] The *pronoetai* on the lower tier of the Apion estate, who collected billon and kind from rural populations but made payments in gold, faced precisely the same situation. Webber and Wildavsky further note that tax farmers would "collect in-kind taxes at remote places where taxpayers were ignorant of the market value of their produce. Agents could convert grain into money at less than the going rate, then profit later from its sale."[38] Justinian's *Novel* 128 (545 CE) stipulates that collections in kind be valued at specific prices or according to specific markets, indicating that collectors contemporary with the Apion *pronoetai* were attempting the same activities.[39]

Webber and Wildavsky's description of the *publicani*'s collections in Asia also reveals how control over land expanded and what role longer-term contracts played in that expansion: "Syndicate agents in Roman Asia exacted a tithe of 10 percent of the crop from all landowners, unmercifully and irrespective of personal circumstances. If a landowner could not pay, the syndicate . . . offered to lend funds at interest. . . . When the landowner could not pay tax arrears plus accumulated interest, the tax-farming syndicate confiscated his land."[40] The merciless collection practices are reminiscent of the complaints in *P.Oxy.* 1.130 and 27.2497 from Apion tenants, who described the confiscation of movable property by the *pronoetai* despite the tenants' dire circumstances. In a number of contracts from the Apion dossier, movable and immovable properties were written as collateral against default.[41] *Novels* 32 and 34, from the mid-sixth century, were meant to combat a problem that occurred in certain provinces when small amounts of grain were loaned to farmers against their land: upon default

37. Webber and Wildavsky 1986, 117.
38. Webber and Wildavsky 1986, 118.
39. Novel 128, chapter 1: σημαινούσας τὸ ὁπὸσον ἐν ἑκάστῃ ἐπαρχία ἤτοι πόλει ὑπὲρ ἑκάστου ἰούγου ἢ ἰουλίων ἢ κεντουρίων ἢ ἄλλων οἱωνδήποτε ὀνομάτων τοῦτο μὲν ἐν εἴδει τοῦτο δὲ ἐν χρυσίῳ δημοσίων ἕνεξεν επίκειται, φανερούσας δὲ καὶ τῶν εἰδῶν τὴν ἀποτίμησιν κατὰ τὴν τράπεζαν καὶ τὴν ἐν ἑκαστῳ τόπῳ κρατοῦσαν συνήθειαν, καὶ τί ἐξ αὐτῶν εἰς τὴν ἄρκαν εἰσφερεσθαι ἢ ἐν ἑκάστῃ ἐπαρχίᾳ δίδοσθαι ἢ δαπανᾶσθαι προσήκει.
40. Webber and Wildavsky 1986, 118.
41. E.g., *P.Oxy.* 19.2238, 44.3204, 70.4794.

in desperate times, the farmers would be dispossessed of their property. It is therefore easily conceivable that when tax collections were made by *pronoetai* on lands not owned by the Apions, similar confiscations (and perhaps lending) on behalf of the estate occurred, leading to some expansion of Apion land.

A contributing factor to the merciless collection practices of the *publicani* was the length of the collection contracts on which they bid. Rather than the usual annual bidding, the Asian contracts were extended to five years to compensate for the difficulties of making collections in so remote an area.[42] This removed the check on the *publicani*'s avarice, namely, the possibility that their contract might not be renewed if there were complaints of extortionate collection or collusion in bidding. The *pronoetes* contract *P.Oxy.* 1.136 demonstrates that contracts were annual on the lower tier of the Apion estate. But the consistency of the areas of collection found in the Apion accounts suggests that collection agreements made on the upper tier were longer term.[43]

State Bureaucracy and Tax Farming: Ptolemaic Egypt

Along with many other Greek institutions, the τελῶναι (tax farmers) were introduced to Egypt at some point after Alexander's conquest.[44] By 259 BCE, the date of *P.Rev.* (an assemblage of regulations governing tax-farming practices),[45] tax farming in some form was widespread there.[46] But that document shows the role of the Ptolemaic τελώνης to have been so limited that he ceased to resemble a tax farmer. Collections were made by local agents who were paid a wage from the nome officials and served at the joint discretion of nome officials and tax farmers,[47] not an unusual situation for a large-scale collection effort. But the

42. Webber and Wildavsky 1986, 117.
43. This point is elaborated on later in this chapter, in connection with the French tax-farming system.
44. Monson (2012, 218 and n. 52) argues against Greek origins for tax farming in Egypt, pointing to evidence of participation by Egyptians in the Ptolemaic system, priests farming temple revenue in Egypt and Babylon, and Egyptian priests' involvement in revenue collection under the Persians. On tax and revenue collection under the Persians, largely an adoption of policies already in place, see Manning 2009, 24–26; Briant 2002, 388–421.
45. Trismegistos no. 8859. *P.Brit.Mus.* 1.10528 may attest tax farming by the Greeks in Egypt as early as 291, but Manning (2009, 152 n. 138) sees no evidence suggesting tax farming over other types of collection in that document.
46. Bingen 2007, 160. On tax farms in Hellenistic Egypt, see Préaux 1939, 450–59; Manning 2009, chapter 5, especially pp. 152–57; Monson 2012, 209–46. On *P.Rev.*, see Bingen's revised edition in *SB Beiheft* 1 (1952); Préaux 1939, especially 65–111, 165–81; Bingen 2007, 157–88; Thompson 2008, 25–38, especially 32–33.
47. Youtie 1967, 13–14.

tax farmer was also supervised by a wage employee of the state, the ἔφορος,[48] and the tax farmer had no independent recourse if someone failed to pay.[49] Making no collections and having little authority over collectors or taxpayers, the tax farmer's role was limited to "fix[ing] the amount of the tax, control[ling] the collection and accounting, and determin[ing] whether the total was greater or smaller than the amount bid."[50] Préaux argues that the system of tax farming manifest in Ptolemaic Egypt was therefore mostly a terminological veneer over the direct collections carried out by the centralized monarchical bureaucracy and that the tax farmers were an essentially useless part of a Greek system grafted onto the existing Egyptian one.[51]

Bingen attributes the persistence of the veneer to a lack of imagination on the part of the conquering Greeks, who conceived of no other way to make collections of indirect taxes.[52] He concedes that the tax farmers were assigned the further role of "insuring for the kings benefit against financial risks," but he writes that "it is unthinkable that the first Ptolemies deliberately gave only this role, and such a limited role, to the tax farming companies."[53] This assessment, however, underestimates the value of tax farmers, who oiled the gears of the fiscal machinery in a world before central banking. Manning writes that the Ptolemaic taxation system's "complexity, and the competitiveness of tax farming arrangements . . . served the interest of the king by creating new organizations within the state that prevented collective action against him."[54] He continues, "The auction process . . . may have functioned as a recruiting device to bring persons into the bureaucratic structure."[55] Moreover, tax farming is unique among the collection systems in that it gives the state access to capital from taxes in anticipation of collection, allows for a predictable income, and lays much of the risk at the feet of collectors. The *publicani* and the French tax-farming system (discussed below) also show that tax farmers could act as clearinghouses for the state, eliminating the need to transport bulky or highly valuable goods to a centralized location before redistributing them back from where they came.[56] Under a strict wage or share system, these properties do not read-

48. Youtie 1967, 14.
49. Youtie 1967, 14.
50. Bingen 2007, 164.
51. Préaux 1939, 450–51.
52. Bingen 2007, 167.
53. Bingen 2007, 166–67. On this role of the τελώνης, see Rostotvzeff 1941, 320–30.
54. Manning 2009, 142.
55. Manning 2009, 156, citing Eisenstadt 1993, 129.
56. Webber and Wildavsky 1986, 117; Matthews 1958, 12–13.

ily arise for the state to exploit. The Ptolemaic example therefore shows that a tax-farming system might coexist with a state collection bureaucracy, much as the Apion collection system functioned within the state collection apparatus extending from Constantinople. Thompson describes the relationship between the tax farmers and the state bureaucracy as mutually reinforcing: "Collection rights were auctioned on a specified occasion and the guarantees provided by the successful tax-farmers served to ensure the revenues of the crown, while the regular royal officials in post provided the lists of taxpayers and helped in recording the process."[57]

The French Tax-Farming System

The development of the French tax collection system from the late Middle Ages to the eighteenth century provides an explanatory model for the transition from the fourth-century method, evident in the Papnouthis and Dorotheos archive, to the system in place under the Apions.[58] This section offers a description of the French system, a discussion of points of contact with the Apion estate's relationship with its collectors and the state, and a possible explanation for the expansion of the area for which the Apion estate collected taxes.[59] The French system provides a particularly apt comparison to the Apion estate, because it was largely agricultural, involved a wealthy elite with connections to a central government located in a remote capital city, was used in a period of expanding importance of money taxes and heavy state expenditure, operated on multiple tiers, and existed alongside a robust state bureaucracy. Because the French system and the Apion estate share many critical features, inferences about the Apion estate can be made from the more detailed understanding available to us for the French system.

Revenue Farming and Tax Farming

Tax farming was used extensively in France from the late Middle Ages through the eighteenth century. It grew out of the revenue farming practiced by landholding aristocrats, as money income associated with the lands they owned

57. Thompson 2008, 31–32.
58. Some material from this section is expanded on in McConnell, forthcoming.
59. For an overview of the French system, see Matthews 1958.

increased. Land was leased out, granting the lessee rights to the produce grown on the land. The other rights associated with the land—tolls, rent on structures, and other dues—also fell under rental contracts.[60] Like tax farmers, revenue farmers assumed potential risks and profits; like the state, the landowner ensured himself a steady revenue, unburdened himself of administrative chores, and potentially benefited from payment in advance of collection. The basis of the revenue farms in France was sometimes a marketable surplus of produce, which made the revenue farmer essentially a tenant farmer.[61] More often, however, the basis lay in the money charges associated with owning the land. Land owned by the monarch was managed in this same way, and taxes were eventually among the money charges owed on such land. The collection of taxes was treated in the same way as the collection of other revenues. On royal land, "the legal relation between a tax-farmer and the king was the same as the relation between a revenue-farmer and the proprietor of an estate."[62]

In the French revenue-farming system, the rights to individual tolls or dues could be farmed out separately so that different farmers might have collection rights over the same piece of land. Taxes, one of the revenue sources associated with a piece of land, fell into a special category because not the landowner but the state retained the ultimate tax rights over the produce of the land. Tax farmers made collections on three classes of land: state-owned land, land they owned themselves, and land owned by others. On state-owned land, the possessor of the tax rights was identical to the possessor of the rights to other revenues, eliminating any meaningful distinction between taxes and other revenues collected. Outside of state land, ownership—the ability to benefit directly from or to farm out rights to the produce, tolls, and dues—was divorced from tax rights, which the state alone had the ability to farm out. Where the tax farmer was the also the landowner—that is, where the landowner had won the bid for the right to collect taxes associated with his own land—the situation was akin to state-owned land: taxes were not distinguishable in any meaningful way from other revenues. A tax farmer might also make collections on land owned by a third party without alienating him from his other rights to the land. In that case, the tax farmer treated the rented tax rights over a neighbor's land the same as any other revenue source over which he had rights.

60. In Roman Egypt, a rent contract could include the right to sell water raised by mechanical irrigators installed on the property. See, e.g., *P.Ross.Georg.* 2.19 (141 CE).

61. Matthews 1958, 6.

62. Matthews 1958, 7.

All three situations have analogues to collections made by the Apions. The *pronoetes* accounts provide evidence that the Apions held tax-farming contracts for land they owned and that they collected certain taxes from neighboring landowners. The non-tax rights to land in the former category were also held by the Apions, so that they rented out the rights to the produce (tenant farming) and the other productive assets on the land (e.g., mills, oil presses, and dovecotes), along with the tax collection rights.[63] Once the payment to the state for the rights of tax collection had been settled, all the collections they made on this land were bound for the same coffers, irrespective of whether the right was for taxes or for other revenues. As in the French system, taxes collected from neighbors were treated similarly to their other revenues. The example in *P.Oxy.* 55.3804.92 of Isaac son of Melas, who pays the Apions ὑπὲρ ἰδίας γῆς (for private land), makes this clear.[64] *P.Oxy.* 16.1915 reveals that the Apions administered imperial land, collecting taxes and other revenues from those associated with the land accounted for in the document. In this case, the state farmed out to the Apions not only its tax rights but also rights to its other revenues. The Apions then incorporated the state-owned land into their larger collection apparatus.

A large estate collecting the revenues produced on its land would face the same choice among systems that a state faced in the collection of taxes. The circumstances under which states farmed out taxes are the same as those under which estates established agricultural tenancy rather than direct management of the land. Many of the determining factors were largely the same: when land was managed directly (i.e., when a wage system was used), laborers did not have an immediate incentive to maximize yields,[65] and monitoring was necessary to ensure that laborers did not sell produce on the side for their own profit. Under a rent system, monitoring of labor was unnecessary, since cultivators were self-interested and since payment to the landowner was independent of productivity.[66] Sarris argues that the Apion estate mostly managed its land directly under a wage system, using a rental system only as

63. Several such examples are in *P.Oxy.* 55.3804.

64. Taxes collected on a neighbor's land would be treated like other revenues to which the Apions were entitled. Consider, for example, an estate renting oxen to its neighbors. Simply because the estate did not own the land on which the oxen were used, we would not expect them to treat the income generated from renting those oxen differently from rent gotten from lessees renting oxen for use on estate land.

65. The wage was not dependent on the yield.

66. The owner was paid a negotiated sum based on anticipated yield, and the contracted cultivators were motivated to maximize yield because their remuneration was the amount in excess of the negotiated sum.

a supplement. While he overemphasizes the role of such direct management, clearly at least some Apion land was exploited directly, especially on orchards and vineyards adjacent to the large house the Apions kept, known as the προάστιον ἔξω τῆς πύλης.[67] Most of the land associated with the Apion estate was not contiguous but distributed throughout the nome. In light of the relative advantages and disadvantages of direct exploitation versus a rental system, it is plausible that those lands nearest to the center of operations and therefore most easily monitored were exploited directly, whereas the farther-flung lands were under rental agreements. The point of emphasis is that once the estate acquired a tax-farming contract, that contract became a revenue source much like any other. There is no reason, therefore, to suppose that a different system of collection was used for taxes than for other types of revenue on the Apion estate. If, as was argued in chapter 2, Sarris' arguments about the role of the *autourgia* are overstated and if the produce from land was exploited chiefly through leasing, it should follow that tax collection on the lower tier was also carried out through a rental system.

Credit

Under the French system, tax farmers provided credit to the state through different mechanisms increasing in complexity over the centuries. The most straightforward provision of credit was payment of all or part of the money bid for the right of tax collection before completion of the actual collection. Tax farmers would pay the state the bid price in regular intervals over the course of the year but would collect much more sporadically, sometimes taking three to four calendar years to collect a single year's taxes.[68] The state additionally required a deposit from the collector in case of default, money that could be used by the state immediately. These practices are similar to those of the lower level of the Apion estate. The *pronoetai* were required to provide a deposit once given the right of collection. This deposit functioned as interest on the "loan" (i.e., the right to collect taxes to which the Apions were entitled) extended to the collectors on the lower tier. Furthermore, the deposit provided the estate with an infusion of immediately available capital. Like the payments made by the French tax farmers, the *pronoetai* paid the Apions in regularly scheduled installments

67. This "house outside the gate" is attested in *P.Oxy.* 16.1925, *PSI* 3.193, and *P.Wisc.* 2.66.
68. Matthews 1958, 11, 28.

throughout the year.[69] Ruffini argues that such regular payments also occurred on the upper tier, from the estate to the state.[70]

As the French state began to rely increasingly on the farms to provide credit, the scale of tax farms increased. Whereas tax farming was "fragmented" in its early incarnation, with each tax farmed under a different contract by a different contractor, "both the government and the financiers felt the need for larger, more centralized tax-farming units embracing all taxes of similar type levied upon a province rather than a parish or upon the entire kingdom rather than upon separate parishes."[71] The larger units could be administered more efficiently, by reducing overlapping bureaucracies; they could be managed more easily by the state; and "above all, such large tax-farms served as more adequate bases for the manipulation of the credit potentialities of the tax farming system."[72]

The most significant such "credit potentiality" was the system under which tax farmers would accept collection rights for future years in exchange for honoring the state's requests for local expenditure in excess of the current year's collection revenues. In many cases, tax farmers acted as clearinghouses facilitating the payment of locally incurred expenses. The use of tax farmers in the French system avoided the need to transport large quantities of coins long distances and then back to make local payments. The Apion *pronoetes* accounts show that a similar function was carried out on the lower tier of the estate, with the *pronoetai* noting expenditures as remissions from their collection. This practice avoided the need for making all the collections, handing them to a central office, and then making all expenditures separately. Before the advent of banknotes, such clearinghouses were crucial to the fiscal operation of states, and the *publicani* also played this important role in the Roman Republic.[73] In the French system, the tax farmer was instructed to disperse money owed by the state and could thus deduct that amount from the bid promised to the state for the right to collect. As the French state incurred more and more costs, the amount of the local expenditures asked of the tax farmers outsized the amount the tax farmers owed the state for the bids. The tax farmers were thus required to dip into their own funds or to acquire more funds on credit. As a result, hav-

69. The schedules on which their payments were made are noted at the ends of the expenditure sections in the accounts (e.g., *P.Oxy.* 55.3804.275–81).
70. Ruffini 2008, 105–6. See also chapter 4 of the present study.
71. Matthews 1958, 38.
72. Matthews 1958, 38.
73. Webber and Wildavsky 1986, 117.

ing a certain level of capital on hand was essential to their ability to provide the state with credit.

But the French tax farmers depended to some extent on their ability to obtain credit for themselves from private citizens, who were, as Azabou and Nugent have noted, understandably wary of lending money directly to a sovereign.[74] As discussed in chapter 4, Papnouthis and Dorotheos exercised a similar intermediary function. The Apions also had relationships with bankers but were able to use different means to obtain credit, which could then be extended to the state. Issuing *pittakia* (a type of scrip) in lieu of payment enabled the estate to consider as paid off those they owed payment to, without having transferred any real money to them, thereby obtaining a form of credit from those over whom they exercised control as landlord or tax farmer. As compensation for their extension of credit, French tax farmers obtained collection rights for future years over greater areas at rent that had been lowered according to the level of debt incurred by the state. As the debt requirements of the state increased, rights for collection could be extended further into the future, the area over which a particular collector had rights could be expanded, or both. By honoring these expenditures in excess of the bid, the tax farmers were providing credit to the state. In the course of its development from the late Middle Ages through the eighteenth century, the quasi-national bank function of large tax farmers was fully realized, and the provision of credit to the state came to be emphasized over collection functions. Providing the state with credit became more commonplace, and the umbrella of tax collection for which the French tax farmers were responsible expanded.[75]

During the same period as the Apion expansion, the state was engaged in numerous costly undertakings, and its finances were severely strained.[76] Expansion similar to that undergone by the French tax-farming companies, owing to the increasing importance of their role in making credit available to the state, offers an explanation for the rapid expansion of the number of *prostasiai* comprising the Apion collection umbrella during the sixth century. In chapter 3, it was demonstrated that the expansion was from wider ownership, a greater

74. Azabou and Nugent 1988, 686.
75. Similarities to the French revenue system further explain why the Apion estate did not distinguish between the collections it made from leases and those made from taxes. Just as we would not expect a French revenue farmer to make careful distinctions between the money collected for tolls and the money collected for rent, we should not expect the Apions to separate lease revenue from taxes, which were just another revenue source associated with the land. One of the reasons there was little distinction made between tax revenue and other kinds of revenue was that there was little practical distinction between these revenues once the contract for collection had been awarded.
76. See chapter 4; Cameron 2000, 84.

area of fiscal responsibility on the part of the Apions, or both. If the Apion estate's role in providing credit to the state was attendant on its role in tax farming, a rapid expansion of its area of fiscal responsibility might be explained.

Managing Cash Flow on Multiple Tiers

The French system used distinct apparatuses for the collection of direct and indirect taxes. For direct taxes, a two-tiered system was in place. The lower tier, called the "financial receivers," retained a fixed proportion of collections and then passed the remainder to the upper tier, called the "general receivers," who retained a fixed proportion before passing on the remainder to the state treasury.[77] On its face, the collection of direct taxes was a share system on both tiers. But to ensure predictable and regular revenue, the state initiated a rent system, with the general receivers (the upper tier) advancing the anticipated tax revenue, less 4 to 5 percent, to the treasury. In effect, then, the upper tier operated on a rent system, the lower tier on a share system. It is significant that the upper tier of the French system was able to advance the state money in anticipation of the actual collection of the taxes by the lower tier. Tax anticipation depended on the general receivers' possession of sufficient capital and ability to obtain credit from others with capital. This is precisely the situation described for the two tiers of the Apion estate: the estate's capital reserves, inflated by delaying payment of their own private debts, could bear payment of the bid price in anticipation of collection by the lower tier. That flexibility allowed the estate to profit from its arrangement with the state, expand the area over which it had collection rights, and extract still further profit from the speculative activities of the *pronoetai,* once collections were finally made. The problem for the upper Apion tier, as for the French general receivers, became one of managing cash flow. Once sufficient capital had been accumulated to ensure credit, the Apion estate could withstand the outlay of money to the state in anticipation of collection and, in exchange, could see a return on such loans in the long term, generating further capital. The expansion of the entire enterprise was self-reinforcing.

Lease Length

By the seventeenth century, the French system was characterized by the sale of heritable collection offices. In other words, leases had become perpetual. Mat-

---

77. Matthews 1958, 27–28.

thews argues that this venality had a dual purpose. First, it was a way for the state to obtain money quickly, as illustrated by the fact that the collection rights were sold to different collectors for alternating years, so that more than one office could be sold to cover a particular tax in an area. But the sale of heritable collection offices also acted as a barrier to entry, ensuring that only those with sufficient wealth and credit of their own would be relied on by the state for the provision of credit. On the lower level, the payments required of the Apion *pronoetai* would have fulfilled the same purpose as the sale of offices, restricting the position of collector to those who could actually be made accountable for amounts in arrears. Absent this, the reallocation of risk to the *pronoetai* would be a mirage.

Long-term leases of collection rights, similar to those that heritable venal offices brought about in France, are a strong likelihood on the upper tier of the Apion estate. As noted above, the consistency of the *epoikia* for which the Apion estate had collection responsibilities in *P.Oxy.* 16.1911 and 55.3804 indicates at least very long-term leases on the upper tier. *P.Oxy.* 16.1915 (557) shows that the Apions administered imperial land, making collections and expenditures according to their *apaitesima*. Many of the entries in that document are described as being done ἐξ ἀρχαιωθ(έντος) καὶ ἀμνημονεύτου χρόνου, "according to the ancient way and from time immemorial."[78] Moreover, as Hickey argues, the land classed as *apotakton chorion* was vine land owned by the church or the state but administered by the Apions.[79] Administration of this land would have involved collection of revenues, including taxes. Based on *P.Cair. Masp.* 3.67299.39–40, Gascou identified *apotakton* with *emphuteusis*, a type of perpetual lease.[80] Hickey argues, in contrast, that they are not identical and that the *emphuteusis* is a type of *apotakton*.[81] In either case, the *apotakton* was a long-term lease, sometimes even perpetual, in which the Apions were engaged for the collection of taxes.

Because leases of tax farms were for large areas and long periods in France, determining their price by competitive auction became untenable.[82] Instead, all major tax farms were "awarded as a result of direct secret negotiations between

---

78. See Hickey 2012, 52–58, on the Apion administration of imperial land, especially *apotakton chorion*. On the date of *P.Oxy.* 16.1915, see Mazza 2001, 24 n. 73.
79. Hickey 2012, 53–58.
80. Gascou 1985, 7–8.
81. Hickey 2012, 53–58.
82. Matthews 1958, 40–41.

the financiers and the finance ministers."[83] This practice offers another possible scenario for the Apions, who, like the French tax farmers, were engaged on long-term or perpetual leases, so that competitive auctions were no longer possible as a means of setting the rent price. The closeness of the Apions with the imperial family in the fifth and sixth centuries also argues in favor of backroom dealings comparable to those of France. The objects of such direct negotiations would certainly have been money, but, again, the closeness of the Apions with the imperial family and their political prominence, culminating in the ordinary consulship of Apion II in 539, suggest that official honors were on offer as well.

The examples given so far offer two possible explanations for a shift toward longer-term leases on tax farms in Byzantine Egypt. When the *publicani* were granted the right to collect on Asian taxes, leases were extended to five years to account for the difficulties of operating so far from Rome; that is, for assuming greater risk, the *publicani* were compensated with greater security in their position and a longer period in which to deal with variance in collection.[84] For the French tax farmers, longer leases were granted as a way for the state to borrow against its future revenues. In both cases, offering longer-term contracts was a way for the state to use its future tax rights as negotiating leverage in the present. That the Apions came to enjoy very long-term leases over tax rights indicates that the state was behaving in a similar way in their case. Absent any obvious assumption of additional risk by the Apions, the French example supplies credit provision to the state as a plausible reason.

The Value of Tax Farmers beyond Collection

In Ptolemaic Egypt, the noncollection-related roles played by tax farmers, including their ability to provide credit to the state and act as clearinghouses, made them valuable even when circumstances made other systems preferable for tax collection. Matthews points out that in seventeenth-century France, there were not barriers to eliminating tax farming as the means of collection; indeed, in some years, the tax-farming leases were refused, and salaried government officials took over administration of collections.[85] But because the use of salaried government officials reduced the availability of tax anticipation

83. Matthews 1958, 40–41.
84. On a short-term lease, a poor year could be disastrous. On a longer-term lease, a poor year was more likely to be offset by a good year, thereby flattening the impact of variance.
85. Matthews 1958, 18.

through credit, the state consistently tried to return to the farming system. The French tax-farming companies' management of the collection bureaucracy, the *service à la régie*, was subordinate to its financial role, or *service du trésor*. Therefore, "the *raison d'être* of the eighteenth-century Company of General Farmers was its skill in manipulating the credit possibilities of a tax-farming lease, . . . its *service du trésor*."[86]

In the absence of central banking, the services that groups of cash-rich individuals could provide to the state through tax farming were, as shown by the cases of Athens, Ptolemaic Egypt, republican Rome, and early modern France, too appealing to pass up when need for money arose. Providing those services to the state often proved highly lucrative. Since many of the same circumstances existed in Byzantine Egypt as in those other milieus, it is plausible that the Apions and their peers in Egypt also fulfilled a dual mandate: to manage the collection of taxes and facilitate tax anticipation. In early modern France, the financial possibilities emerged from a simpler apparatus devoted primarily to facilitating tax collection, but as the apparatus became greater in scale and complexity, the collectors' role in financing the state through credit also grew. In Egypt, it is possible to trace a very similar trajectory from collectors like Papnouthis and Dorotheos in the fourth century to the Apions in the sixth. Absent signs of productive surplus and extensive market engagement, the financial function of tax farming is also an explanation for the Apions' enrichment.

The Coexistence of Tax-Farming and State Collection Bureaucracy

The laws and the papyri give the impression of a dizzying array of minor officials working in the tax bureaucracy of the Byzantine Empire. Different taxes, regions, and time periods all saw different officials involved at some level of fiscal administration. Where the semipublic tax-farming operations like the Apions' might fit in with these government institutions can be difficult to envision. The French General Farms provide a picture of how the public and semipublic can operate together. Matthews draws a distinction between the institution of the French General Farms—the tax rights and the bureaucracy—and the Company of General Farmers—financiers who assumed the dual role of managing the General Farms and financing the state. Of the former, Matthews writes, "as a bureaucracy, the General Farms possessed the equipment, the per-

86. Matthews 1958, 17.

sonnel, and the procedural routines to perform this function without regard to the purely tax farming relation that existed between the government and the Company of General Farmers."[87] It consisted of "a considerable corpus of standing rules and regulations sanctioned by the king, and a huge body of personnel, the most important members of which were permanently employed royal officers, directly employed by the king."[88]

Both the French example and that of Ptolemaic Egypt show that an extensive state bureaucracy and a private collection apparatus are not mutually exclusive. To a point, a similar coexistence might be posited for the Byzantine system of collection: the state retained a collection apparatus, and the Apion estate managed and financed collection and tax anticipation. So, for example, the Apion *pronoetai* made their grain collections and handed over the *embole* to the *embolator*, a state bureaucrat. But for the Apions, the collection bureaucracy at the lowest levels was entirely within the estate's control. Ptolemaic Egypt and early modern France demonstrate that even where there is plentiful state involvement in the collection of taxes, tax farmers can play an important or even predominant role in the collection, operating alongside and within the state bureaucracy.

Chapter 4 ended by characterizing the relationship between the state and the upper tier of the Apion estate as one of parties in a negotiation. Matthews describes the relationship between the French monarchy and the tax-farming companies similarly: "The royal controller-general did not, and could not, command the General Receivers and the General Farmers as subordinates. Rather he negotiated with them seeking not obedience but bargaining advantages."[89] In language reminiscent of Gascou's description of the Apion estates, Matthews continues, "the General Receivers and General Farmers were not modern civil servants, but chiefs of quasiprivate financial corporations."[90] The parallels between the Apions and the French system suggest that the Apion estates might also have been used "as instruments of financial manipulation . . . dedicated to the policy of tax anticipation" and that their main importance to the government was "not their managerial or administrative skill, but their financial strength and willingness to place at the king's disposal their own private credit."[91]

87. Matthews 1958, 16.
88. Matthews 1958, 16.
89. Matthews 1958, 31.
90. Matthews 1958, 32–33.
91. Matthews 1958, 32–33.

Conclusion

Highlighting the points of comparison between the Apion estate's tax and revenue collection apparatus and other historical instances of tax farming can help to fill in gaps in our understanding of estates in Byzantine Egypt. The Apion system of collection emerged from the consolidation of dispersed, small-scale, independent collectors like Papnouthis and Dorotheos into syndicates controlled by the wealthiest and most influential members of local society.[92] After this consolidation, the Apion estate employed collection subcontractors, drawn from the bureaucratic apparatus already in place for the private functions associated with estate management and non-tax revenue farming, such as land leasing and equipment rental.

The Apions owned a large amount of land around Oxyrhynchus. A number of different valuable assets were associated with that land: the produce grown on it, mills and presses installed on it, and animals working it. The three systems of tax collection discussed in chapter 4 are specific applications of systems of collection *simpliciter*, equally applicable to taxes, tolls, agricultural crops, and anything else producing valuables. The methods available to the Apions to exploit the land and other assets they controlled therefore track with those available to them for tax collection. They could hire workers to reap the produce and collect it directly, they could lease the land for a fixed amount based on the expected amount that the land would generate, or they could use sharecropping. Sarris argues that direct exploitation was the most significant means of revenue collection and that leasing was supplementary; but, as I argued in chapter 2, little evidence suggests that direct exploitation was more prevalent than leasing. The use of *apaitesima* and the handful of lease contracts indicate, at the very least, the existence of a bureaucratic apparatus for collections under a rent system.[93] The state also possessed taxation rights over this same land and the people working it and was faced with the same options for exploiting it. According to some contractual arrangement,[94] the state leased to the Apions tax collection rights over much of the land around Oxyrhynchus—both land owned and land not owned by the Apions. Once the tax rights came into the possession of the Apion family, they were treated no differently from any of the other valuable

92. Bagnall 1993, 158–60.
93. *P.Oxy.* 16.2037 is an *apaitesimon*; *P.Flor.* 3.325 and *P.Oxy.* 63.4390 (both Apion) and *P.Oxy.* 6.913 (non-Apion) are leases.
94. E.g., *P.Oxy.* 16.1915.

assets associated with the estate. They were incorporated into the existing mechanisms of revenue collection, most prominently through tax farming. Much as there was an administrative layer determining where irrigation machinery, mills, and oil presses were to be installed and how collections were to be made from them, there was an administrative tier, above the rest of the revenue-farming apparatus, that contracted with the state, secured the right of tax collection, and handled payments owed to the state. In other words, tax farming was a subset of the category of revenue farming.[95]

To suggest that a rent system of collection was adopted because of the credit it could provide is to attribute more foresight and financial understanding to the Apions and the imperial government than is plausible. More probably, credit became available as a natural result of a rent system adopted for the reasons laid out by Coşgel and Miceli and discussed in chapter 4. The French tax-farming estates can provide particular insight into how Apion tax-farming arrangements were used to finance the state through credit. The financial aspects of the Apion estate's rent contracting for collection increased its influence, especially in times of tumult and war, when the state had a pressing need for cash. The greater reliance of the state on large estates for financing afforded the Apions still greater bargaining power in determining the fees for collection of taxes (i.e., they could lower the rent paid to the state for the right to collect). The increased leverage of collectors like the Apions freed their hands to squeeze the rural population from whom they collected, unchecked by the state, whose interest in protecting the rural population from extortionate behavior was subordinate to its interest in keeping the flow of credit open. The French collection system, specifically how credit was used in it, offers possible explanations for the expansion of land over which the Apions had either ownership or the right of collection. The French and Ptolemaic examples also show how a state bureaucracy devoted to collection can exist alongside and symbiotically with a private tax-farming system like the one described for Byzantine Egypt and likely at work on the Apion estate.

95. Matthews 1958, 4–6.

CHAPTER 6
Conclusion

Hickey's work has shown that the revenues from leased land were insufficient to account for the wealth of the Apion family. Sarris' contention that the *autourgia*, directly managed land, was the source of the family's wealth is insufficiently supported by the evidence. This study therefore asked at the outset what the source of Apion wealth was. The answer posited relates to the Apions' role in tax collection. The core argument consisted of three steps. First was a critique of Sarris' claims concerning the prominent role of the *autourgia* in the production of a marketable surplus. The model offered here aligns with Hickey's contentions that there was little agricultural surplus available for sale on the open market and that the agricultural production of the estates was not managed in a profit-seeking way. Second, it was established, based on contracts and accounts, that the *pronoetai*, the lower-level collectors on the Apion estate, were required to pay the estate in cash and kind in excess of their collection requirements. This excess was shown to have come from speculation in transmuting billon and kind into gold and from the extracurricular extractions that collectors made from the lessees and landowners for whom they were responsible. Third, the possible tax collection arrangements between the state and the estate were outlined, and tax farming emerged as the likeliest of the possibilities. Circumstances that led to tax-farming systems in a number of historically analogous situations were shown to be present also in Byzantine Egypt and on the Apion estate. Their presence strengthens the claim that the relationship between the state and the estate took the form of a tax-farming contract.

The Autourgia

There are flaws in Sarris' bipartite model and his description of the *autourgia* as the most important sector of the estates. Only a handful of documents explicitly mention the *autourgia*, and those are not dispositive in the way Sarris presents them.[1] When the context can be determined, these documents all concern fodder.[2] Sarris, however, expands the corpus of documents referring to the *autourgia* by connecting it with names of location markers (e.g.,"Ἔξω τῆς Πύλης). Wherever those names appear, Sarris infers that the *autourgia* is meant. It is on this land that Sarris finds the wide variety of crops he claims were cultivated on the *autourgia* and tracked in accounts that are no longer extant. If, as I argued in chapter 2, the identification of these location markers with the *autourgia* cannot be supported, the thesis about the role of the *autourgia* in generating wealth for the Apions is significantly undermined. The *autourgia* is clearly associated with fodder, a product that the estate needed to purchase externally and that was therefore unlikely to have been produced for a marketable surplus. The *autourgia* and its association with fodder, along with lease agreements and account entries in which estate-owned animals are used by lessees, suggest that the estate and the lessees associated with the estate maintained animals centrally for transportation and agricultural uses.

The case for the deliberate transfer of labor to the *autourgia*—indicating central direction and profit-seeking behavior—is dubious as well. It is based on the observation that some laborers listed in accounts with a certain *epoikion* (or village) as their *origo* appear associated with another location as well. According to Sarris' argument, this implies that renters were deployed as laborers on a different part of the estate, presumably on the *autourgia*, from the one they rented. Mazza offers other explanations—equally plausible, if not more so—for a cultivator working land other than his *origo*: farmers might rent land in both their own *epoikion* and a neighboring one; or, for various possible reasons, the physical location and the fiscal *origo* might not be one and the same.[3] In chapter 2, I demonstrated that *georgoi* varied greatly in social status, with some owning land and others, perhaps family members of lessees and small landowners, not

---

1. Mazza 2008, 152.
2. Documents connecting the *autourgia* with fodder and listed by Mazza (2008, 152) are *P.Oxy.* 16.1913.36–39; 16.1911.178–80; 55.3804.244–48; 18.2195.132–33. Hickey (2001, 193) points out that the Apion *oikos*' need to buy fodder and seed for fodder indicates that it would not or could not meet its own internal demand for fodder. Hence fodder as a source for profit is unlikely.
3. Mazza 2008, 153.

even leasing land of their own. The presence of *georgoi* who owned and leased land or who worked land owned or leased by others provides an explanation hewing more closely to the evidence than does the contention that there were centrally directed transfers of labor to the scantily documented *autourgia*.

Collection on Two Tiers

The estate accumulated wealth from the methods it used to collect taxes and other revenue from the rural peasantry in Oxyrhynchus.[4] To make these collections, the estate employed local agents who engaged in speculative trade in a gold market, using as principal the collections made in kind and billon from small-scale lessees and landowners. While the type of smoking-gun evidence for gold speculation by Papnouthis and Dorotheos in the fourth century is wanting for Apion agents in the sixth century, a few points can be emphasized in its favor. Because payments made by the *pronoetai* were in gold and because the collections they made were mainly in smaller denominations than the *solidus*, the *pronoetai* had to transmute collections into gold. Moreover, the salary of a *pronoetes* was meager compared to the fee in gold required of him for the privilege of his position. His collections in billon and kind could be put to use in any number of ways in search of a marginal gain for a living. Given the involvement of the *pronoetai* in transmuting collections into gold, the gold markets are a natural place for investment. This is all the more likely given precedent for similar speculation among collectors under a rent system, as can be seen among the *publicani* and other collectors in Roman Egypt. As insurance against a bust year on the gold market, the *pronoetai* could and, according to the papyri, often did make up shortfalls by pressing those from whom they made their collections.

The estate contractually obligated its collectors to pay the estate dues in exchange for the right to collect, thereby deriving benefits from their speculation. This lower-tier system was made possible by the agreements between the upper tier and the state to secure tax collection rights. These agreements were tax-farming contracts wherein the Apion estate could collect more from the peasantry than it had to pay the state for the collection rights. The activities of

4. There is evidence that the Apions also engaged in urban leasing and farmed out its collection. The extent of this type of activity remains uncertain. See *P.Oxy.* 58.3958, a contract for collection on urban property through a farming system.

the estate on the upper tier are mostly inaccessible through papyrological or literary sources, though the estate appears to have been operating under a fiscal shares system as early as 463–64.[5] Chapter 4 provides a means of evaluating the upper-level activities of the Apion estate and their relationship to the more thoroughly documented lower-tier activities, by creating a theoretical framework based on historical methods of tax collection. From this examination of the upper tier, a secondary benefit to the Apions becomes apparent: as the state came to rely on funds being available before collection, a key aspect of tax-farming systems, the Apions' bargaining position with respect to the state was bettered. An improved bargaining position led to agreements for collection over larger areas and for longer terms, phenomena reflected in the better-documented lower tier.

In addition to the major conclusions about the sources of Apion wealth, I argue that a sixth-century expansion of the area over which the estate was responsible for tax collection can be quantitatively demonstrated. The collection numbers on the *prostasia*-level accounts remain relatively constant, whereas the collections for estate-level accounts expand significantly. Therefore, the expansion is owed to an increase in the number of *prostasiai* associated with the estate—by ownership or tax responsibility—rather than to an increase in the level of taxation or production. Combined with Hickey's arguments about the size of the Apion estate, the calculations further suggest that the expansion was not in the amount of land the Apions owned but in the amount of land on which it made collections. This strongly supports Gascou's model and refutes Sarris'. Quantifying the *prostasiai* associated with the estate also permits a calculation of the benefits that the estate derived directly from its contractual arrangements with collectors, on the order of 7 percent of their gross collections.

Comparisons

The Athenian system of tax collection shows the propensity of tax-farming systems to concentrate into the hands of a wealthy elite. Collection under the Roman *publicani* concentrates in the same way and also shows the possibilities that a tax-farming system offers to the state, outside of collecting taxes. Especially significant among these possibilities are the extension of credit and facili-

5. Azzarello 2006, 210.

tation of remote expenditures. The Ptolemaic tax system is an instance in which these possibilities were so valuable to the state that tax farming persisted even when conditions made other systems preferable in purely collection terms. Finally, the French tax collection system in place from the late Middle Ages to the seventeenth century shows how large-scale tax-farming systems could be highly lucrative for the collectors, especially from the extension of credit to the state, and it highlights the connection of credit extension to expansion of the area and to increasing periods for which collection rights were conferred. The French system therefore suggests an explanation for the expansion of the Apion collection area. The French example also shows how a private, multitiered collection system can exist alongside an elaborate state collection bureaucracy.

Limitations and Hazards

When arguments and claims about the economy and society of late antique Egypt are made, it is important to keep in mind the precariousness of the evidence on which they rest. The evidence depends on chance survival and on often arbitrary decisions of many individuals on the long path from Middle Egypt to editions on library shelves. Factors skewing the perception of history extracted from documents include whether certain documents and types of documents ended up spending the centuries in drier or wetter locations; whether they were ever discovered and found their way to universities, museums, and libraries; and whether they were selected for edition and were edited well. Moreover, sitting unedited in museums and libraries (and, indeed, in desert sand) are literally thousands of papyri, any one of which could utterly upend the way this place and time are understood. The evolving picture that Keenan's articles draw of Phoibammon in Aphrodito shows that this hazard is present even in the writing of a highly circumscribed "microhistory," focused on a single person for a few years.[6] So much greater is the risk when broader conclusions—about an entire estate or all of Oxyrhynchus, Egypt, the empire, or the age—are drawn from limited evidence. Therefore, confident assertions of

6. Keenan (2007, 235) writes of his 1980 article, "At the end of the article on Phoibammon I engage in a series of speculations, the riskiest of which was that Phoibammon may have had 'little or no family, possibly therefore only his own mouth to feed.' This was immediately proven wrong by the virtually simultaneous publication of a Phoibammon papyrus in the Vatican Library (*P.Vat.Aphrod.* 10) from which it was clear that Phoibammon had a wife."

fact, even about minor points, are difficult to make in good conscience. Offered here is an attempt to create a coherent accounting of the evidence as it now stands, to supplement the limitations of the evidence with historical analogues, and to give a fair evaluation of the interpretations that have come before. Ideally, it is a plausible theory awaiting and welcoming new evidence and new methods to test its validity.

Appendix
Papyri Referred to in the Text

CPR 19.44
P.Amh. 2.79
P.Bagnall 33.10
P.Berl.Zill. 7
P.Brit.Mus. 1.10528
P.Cair. 67057
P.Cair.Masp. 2.67170
P.Cair.Masp. 3.67299
P.Cair.Zen. 1.59004
P.Col. 8.244
P.Dubl. 32
P.Dubl. 33
P.Fay. 34
P.Flor. 3.280
P.Flor. 3.325
P.Iand. 63
P.Laur. 3.75
P.Lond. 2.393
P.Lond. 5.1689
P.Lond. 5.1693
P.Lond. 5.1770
P.Mert. 2.96
*P.Mich.*11.611
*P.Mich.*14.680
P.Michael. 34
P.Oxy. 1.44
P.Oxy. 1.125
P.Oxy. 1.126
P.Oxy. 1.127
P.Oxy. 1.127 *recto*
P.Oxy. 1.130
P.Oxy. 1.135
P.Oxy. 1.136
P.Oxy. 1.138
P.Oxy. 1.144
P.Oxy. 6.913
P.Oxy. 14.1734
P.Oxy. 16.1214
P.Oxy. 16.1831
P.Oxy. 16.1866
P.Oxy. 16.1867
P.Oxy. 16.1895
P.Oxy. 16.1907
P.Oxy. 16.1908
P.Oxy. 16.1909
P.Oxy. 16.1909 *verso*
P.Oxy. 16.1910
P.Oxy. 16.1911

P.Oxy. 16.1912
P.Oxy. 16.1913
P.Oxy. 16.1914
P.Oxy. 16.1915
P.Oxy. 16.1918
P.Oxy. 16.1918 *verso*
P.Oxy. 16.1925
P.Oxy. 16.1939
P.Oxy. 16.1940
P.Oxy. 16.1952
P.Oxy. 16.1968 (= *SB* 26.16722)
P.Oxy. 16.2012
P.Oxy. 16.2020
P.Oxy. 16.2027
P.Oxy. 16.2032
P.Oxy. 16.2033
P.Oxy. 16.2037
P.Oxy. 18.2195
P.Oxy. 18.2195 *verso*
P.Oxy. 18.2196 *verso*
P.Oxy. 18.2204
P.Oxy. 19.2196 *verso*
P.Oxy. 19.2238
P.Oxy. 19.2239
P.Oxy. 19.2243a
P.Oxy. 27.2478
P.Oxy. 27.2479
P.Oxy. 44.3204
P.Oxy. 48.3387
P.Oxy. 48.3393
P.Oxy. 48.3394
P.Oxy. 48.3400
P.Oxy. 48.3401
P.Oxy. 48.3406
P.Oxy. 48.3407
P.Oxy. 48.3417
P.Oxy. 48.3419
P.Oxy. 48.3888
P.Oxy. 50.4584
P.Oxy. 50.4585
P.Oxy. 50.4586
P.Oxy. 55.3803
P.Oxy. 55.3804
P.Oxy. 58.3955
P.Oxy. 58.3958
P.Oxy. 63.4390
P.Oxy. 67.4615
P.Oxy. 70.4790
P.Oxy. 70.4791
P.Oxy. 70.4794
P.Oxy. 71.4831
P.Oxy. 72.4922
P.Oxy. 72.4926
P.Oxy. 72.4927
P.Oxy. 72.4928
P.Oxy. 72.4929
P.Oxy. 8.1130
P.Rev.
P.Ross.Georg. 2.19
PSI 3.193
P.Wash.Univ. 2.102
P.Wisc. 2.66
P.Yale 3.3
SPP 10.111

Glossary

analomata	The expenditures in the accounts.
autourgia	A category of land mostly associated with fodder. Sarris characterizes it as the economic engine of the estates, producing a large surplus sold at market.
edaphos	A division of land; perhaps a division *autourgia*, but the evidence is unclear.
emphuteusis	A permanent lease of state or church land with an upfront payment and low annual payments.
epoikion	Small settlements, often translated as hamlets, in which cultivators of land associated with the Apions lived.
ktema	Land leased by inhabitants of *epoikia*.
lemmata	The collections (or target collections) in the accounts.
pronoetes	An employee of the estate responsible for the collection of taxes and other revenues from a *prostasia*.
prostasia	An administrative division of the estate's collection area comprising five to seven *epoikia* and the associated *ktemata*, overseen by a *pronoetes*.

Bibliography

Andreades, Andreas Michael. *A History of Greek Public Finance*. Cambridge: Harvard University Press, 1933.

Azabou, Mongi, and Jefferey Nugent. "Contractual Choice in Tax Collection Activities: Some Implications of the Experience with Tax Farming." *Journal of Institutional and Theoretical Economics* 144 (1988): 684–705.

Azzarello, Giuseppina. "P. Oxy. XVI 2039 e la nascita della *domus gloriosa* degli Apioni." *Zeitschrift für Papyrologie und Epigraphik* 155 (2006): 207–28.

Azzarello, Giuseppina. *Il dossier della* domus divina *in Egitto*. Berlin: De Gruyter, 2012.

Badian, E. *Publicans and Sinners: Private Enterprise in the Service of the Roman Republic, with a Critical Bibliography*. Ithaca: Cornell University Press, 1983.

Bagnall, Roger S. "Landholding in Late Roman Egypt: The Distribution of Wealth." *Journal of Roman Studies* 82 (1992): 128–49.

Bagnall, Roger S. *Egypt in Late Antiquity*. Princeton: Princeton University Press, 1993.

Bagnall, Roger S. *The Demography of Roman Egypt*. Cambridge: Cambridge University Press, 1994.

Bagnall, Roger S. "The Date of P.Kell I G. 62 and the Meaning of χωρίον." *Chronique d'Égypte* 74 (1999): 329–33.

Bagnall, Roger S. "Village and City: Geographies of Power in Byzantine Egypt." In *Les villages dans l'Empire byzantin*, edited by Jacques Lefort, Cécile Morrisson, and Jean-Pierre Sodini, 553–65. Paris: Buchet-Chastel, 2005.

Bagnall, Roger S., ed. *Egypt in the Byzantine World, 300–700*. Cambridge: Cambridge University Press, 2007.

Bagnall, Roger S. "Village Landholding at Aphrodito in Comparative Perspective." In *Les archives de Dioscore d'Aphrodité cent ans après leur découverte: Histoire et culture dans l'Égypte byzantine; Actes du Colloque de Strasbourg, 8–10 décembre 2005*, edited by J.-L. Fournet, 181–90. Paris: De Boccard, 2008.

Bagnall, Roger, et al. *Consuls of the Later Roman Empire*. Atlanta: Scholars Press, 1987.

Banaji, Jairus. "The Circulation of Gold as an Index of Prosperity in the Central and Eastern Mediterranean in Late Antiquity." In *Coin Finds and Coin Use in the Roman World: The Thirteenth Oxford Symposium on Coinage and Monetary History*, edited by C. E. King and D. G. Wigg, 41–53. Studien zu Fundmünzen der Antike 10. Berlin: Gebrüder Mann Verlag, 1996.

Banaji, Jairus. "Agrarian History and the Labour Organisation of Byzantine Large Estates." In *Agriculture in Egypt: From Pharaonic to Modern Times*, edited by Alan K. Bowman and E. Rogan, 193–216. Oxford: Oxford University Press, 1999.

Banaji, Jairus. "State and Aristocracy in the Economic Evolution of the Late Empire." In *Production and Public Powers in Antiquity*, edited by E. Lo Cascio and D. Rathbone, 107–17. Cambridge: Cambridge Philological Society, 2000.

Banaji, Jairus. *Agrarian Change in Late Antiquity: Gold, Labour, and Aristocratic Dominance*. Oxford: Oxford University Press, 2001.

Beaucamp, J. "Apion et Praejecta: Hypothèses anciennes et nouvelles données." *Revue des Études Byzantines* 59 (2001): 165–78.

Bell, Harold Idris. "The Byzantine Servile State in Egypt." *Journal of Egyptian Archaeology* 4 (1917): 86–106.

Berkes, Lajos. *Dorfverwaltung und Dorfgemeinschaft in Ägypten von Diokletian zu den Abbasiden*. Forthcoming.

Bingen, Jean. *Papyrus Revenue Laws*, nouv. éd. du texte. Sammelbuch griechischer Urkunden aus Ägypten, Beiheft 1. Göttingen: Hubert, 1952.

Bingen, Jean. *Hellenistic Egypt: Monarchy, Society, Economy, Culture*. Edited by Roger Bagnall. Berkeley: University of California Press, 2007.

Bjornlie, M. Shane. Review of *Economy and Society in the Age of Justinian*, by Peter Sarris. BMCR, June 4, 2007. http://bmcr.brynmawr.edu/2007/2007-06-04.html

Bogaert, Raymond. "La banque en Égypte byzantine." *Zeitschrift für Papyrologie und Epigraphik* 116 (1997): 84–140.

Bonneau, Danielle. *Le régime administratif de l'eau du Nil dans l'Égypte grecque, romaine et byzantine*. Leiden: Brill, 1993.

Bowman, Alan K. "Landholding in the Hermopolite Nome in the Fourth Century A.D." *Journal of Roman Studies* 75 (1985): 137–63.

Bowman, Alan K., and E. Rogan. *Agriculture in Egypt: From Pharaonic to Modern Times*. Oxford: Oxford University Press for the British Academy, 1999.

Brass, Tom. "Late Antiquity as Early Capitalism." *Journal of Peasant Studies* 32, no. 1 (2005): 118–50.

Briant, Pierre. *From Cyrus to Alexander: A History of the Persian Empire*. Winona Lake: Eisenbrauns, 2002.

Cameron, Averil, Bryan Ward-Perkins, and Michael Whitby. *The Cambridge Ancient History*. 2nd ed. Vol. 14. Cambridge: Cambridge University Press, 2000.

Cameron, Averil, Bryan Ward-Perkins, and Michael Whitby. *The Cambridge Ancient History*. 2nd ed. Vol. 12. Cambridge: Cambridge University Press, 2005.

Carrié, J. M. "Le 'colonat du Bas-Empire': Un mythe historiographique?" *Opus* 1 (1982): 351–70.

Carrié, J. M.. "Un roman des origines: Les généalogies du 'colonat du Bas-Empire.'" *Opus* 2 (1983): 205–51.

Carrié, J. M.. "Observations sur la fiscalité du IVe siècle pour servir à l'histoire monétaire." In *L'"inflazione" nel quarto secolo D.C.: Atti dell'incontro di studio Roma 1988,* 115–54. Istituto Italiano di Numismatica, 1993.

Christ, Matthew. "The Evolution of the *Eisphora* in Classical Athens." Classical Quarterly 57 (2007): 53–69.

Coase, Ronald H. "The Institutional Structure of Production." Nobel Prize lecture, Stockholm, Sweeden, December 9, 1991. http://www.nobelprize.org/nobel_prizes/economic-sciences/laureates/1991/coase-lecture.html

Conrad, L. I. "Arabic Plague Chronologies and Treatises: Social and Historical Factors in the Formation of a Literary Genre." *Studia Islamica* 54 (1981): 51–93.

Corbier, Mirielle. "Coinage, Society, and Economy." In *The Cambridge Ancient History,* 2nd ed., vol. 12, 393–439. Cambridge University Press, 2005.

Coşgel, M., and T. Miceli. "Tax Collection in History." *Public Finance Review* 37, no. 4 (2009): 399–420.

Cuno, Kenneth M. *The Pasha's Peasants.* Cairo: American University in Cairo Press, 1994.

Decker, Michael. *Tilling the Hateful Earth: Agricultural Production and Trade in the Late Antique East.* Oxford: Oxford University Press, 2009.

Duncan-Jones, R. P. "Variation in Egyptian Grain Measure." *Chiron* 9 (1979): 347–75.

Durliat, Jean. "Les conditions du commerce au VIe siècle." In *The Sixth Century: Production, Distribution, and Demand.* Brill, 1998.

Eastmond, Antony. "Consular Diptychs, Rhetoric, and the Languages of Art in Sixth-Century Constantinople." *Art History* 33, no. 5 (2010): 742–65.

Eisenstadt, Shmuel Noah. *The Political Systems of Empires.* London: Free Press of Glencoe, 1963.

Feissel, Denis, and Jean Gascou. *La pétition à Byzance.* Paris: Association des amis du Centre d'histoire et civilisation de Byzance, 2004.

Finley, Moses I. *The Ancient Economy.* Berkeley: University of California Press, 1973.

Fournet, Jean-Luc. *Les archives de Dioscore d'Aphrodité cent ans après leur découverte: histoire et culture dans l'Égypte byzantine; Actes du Colloque de Strasbourg, 8–10 décembre 2005.* Paris: De Boccard, 2008.

Frank, Tenney. *An Economic History of Rome.* 2nd ed. New York: Cooper Square, 1962.

Gascou, Jean. "De Byzance à l'Islam: Les impôts en Égypte après la conquête arabe." *Journal of the Economic and Social History of the Orient* 26, no. 1 (1983): 97–109.

Gascou, Jean. "Les grands domaines, la cite et l'État en Égypte byzantine: Recherches d'histoire agraire, fiscale et administrative." *Travaux et memoires* 9 (1985): 1–90.

Gascou, Jean. "Les pétitions privées." In *La pétition à Byzance,* edited by Denis Feissel and Jean Gascou, 93–103. Association des amis du Centre d'histoire et civilisation de Byzance, 2004.

Gascou, Jean. *Fiscalité et société en Égypte byzantine*. Bilans de recherche 4. Paris: Association des amis du Centre d'histoire et civilisation de Byzance, 2008.

Gelzer, Matthias. *Studien zur Byzantinischen Verwaltung Ägypten*. Aalen: Quelle und Meyer, 1909.

Gonis, N. "A Late Byzantine Land Lease from Oxyrhynchus: *P.Oxy.* XVI 1968 Revisited." *Tyche* 15 (2000): 93–102.

Gonis, N. "*P.Bingen* 135 and Flavius Apion I." *Zeitschrift für Papyrologie und Epigraphik* 146 (2004): 175–78.

Haldon, John F., ed. *The Social History of Byzantium*. Oxford: Wiley-Blackwell, 2009.

Hardy, Edward Rochie. *The Large Estates of Byzantine Egypt*. New York: Columbia University Press, 1931.

Hickey, Todd Michael. "A Public 'House' but Closed: 'Fiscal Participation' and Economic Decision-Making on the Oxyrhynchite Estate of the Flavii Apiones." PhD diss., University of Chicago, 2001.

Hickey, Todd Michael. "Aristocratic Landholding and the Economy." In *Egypt in the Byzantine World, 300–700*, edited by Roger S. Bagnall, 288–308. Cambridge: Cambridge University Press, 2007.

Hickey, Todd Michael. "An Inconvenient Truth? P.Oxy. 18.2196 verso, the Apion Estate, and *fiscalité* in the Late Antique Oxyrhynchite." *Bulletin of the American Society of Papyrologists* 45 (2008): 87–100.

Hickey, Todd Michael. *Wine, Wealth, and the State in Late Antique Egypt: The House of Apion at Oxyrhynchus*. Ann Arbor: University of Michigan Press, 2012.

Hodges, Richard, and William Bowden. *The Sixth Century: Production, Distribution, and Demand*. Leiden: Brill, 1998.

Janin, Raymond. *Constantinople byzantin: Développement urbain et répertoire topographique*. Paris: Institut français d'Études byzantines, 1964.

Johnson, Allan Chester. *Egypt and the Roman Empire*. Ann Arbor: University of Michigan Press, 1951.

Johnson, Allan Chester, and Louis C. West. *Byzantine Egypt: Economic Studies*. Princeton Studies in Papyrology. Princeton: Princeton University Press, 1949.

Jones, A. H. M. *The Later Roman Empire, 284–602: A Social, Economic, and Administrative Survey*. Norman: University of Oklahoma Press, 1964.

Jones, A. H. M. *The Roman Economy*. Oxford: Blackwell, 1974.

Keenan, James. "Aurelius Phoibammon, Son of Triadelphus: A Byzantine Egyptian Land Entrepreneur." *Bulletin of the American Society of Papyrologists* 17 (1980): 145–54.

Keenan, James. "Aurelius Apollos and the Aphrodite Village Elite." In *Atti del XVII Congresso Internazionale di Papirologia*, 3:957–63. Centro internazionale per lo studio dei papiri ercolanesi, 1984.

Keenan, James. "Papyrology and Byzantine Historiography." *Bulletin of the American Society of Papyrologists* 30 (1993): 137–44.

Keenan, James. Review of *Du village à l'Empire: Autour du Registre fiscal d'Aphroditô (525/526)*, by Constantine Zuckerman. *Bulletin of the American Society of Papyrologists* 42 (2005): 285–97.

Keenan, James. "Byzantine Egyptian Villages." *Egypt in the Byzantine World, 300–700*, edited by Roger S. Bagnall, 226–43. Cambridge University Press, 2007.

Kehoe, Dennis P. *The Economics of Agriculture on Roman Imperial Estates in North Africa*. Göttingen: Vandenhoeck und Ruprecht, 1988.

Kehoe, Dennis P. *Management and Investment on Estates in Roman Egypt during the Early Empire*. Bonn: R. Habelt, 1992.

Kehoe, Dennis P. "Legal Institutions and the Bargaining Power of the Tenant in Roman Egypt." *Archiv für Papyrusforschung* 41, no. 2 (1995): 232–62.

Kehoe, Dennis P. *Investment, Profit, and Tenancy: The Jurists and the Roman Agrarian Economy*. Ann Arbor: University of Michigan Press, 1997.

Kehoe, Dennis P. "Aristocratic Dominance in the Late Roman Agrarian Economy and the Question of Economic Growth." *Journal of Roman Archaeology* 16 (2003): 711–19.

Kehoe, Dennis P. *Law and the Rural Economy in the Roman Empire*. Ann Arbor: University of Michigan Press, 2007.

Kiser, Edgar. "Markets and Hierarchies in Early Modern Tax Systems: A Principal-Agent Analysis." *Politics and Society* 22 (1994): 284–315.

Laniado, A. "Συντελεστής: Notes sur un terme fiscale surinterprété." *Journal of Juridical Papyrology* 26 (1996): 23–51.

Laniado, A. *Recherches sur les notables municipaux dans l'empire protobyzantin*. Travaux et mémoires du Centre de recherche d'histoire et civilisation de Byzance 13. Paris: Association des amis du Centre d'histoire et civilisation de Byzance, 2002.

Levi, Margaret. *Of Rule and Revenue*. Berkeley: University of California Press, 1988.

Liebeschuetz, W. "The Pagarch: City and Imperial Administration in Byzantine Egypt." *Journal of Juridical Papyrology* 18 (1974): 163–68.

Liebeschuetz, W. "Civic Finance in the Byzantine Period: The Laws and Egypt." *Byzantinische Zeitschrift* 89, no. 2 (1996): 389–408.

Lyttkens, Carl Hampus. "Institutions, Taxation, and Market Relationships in Ancient Athens." *Journal of Institutional Economics* 6, no. 4 (2010): 505–27.

Lyttkens, Carl Hampus. *Economic Analysis of Institutional Change in Ancient Greece: Politics, Taxation, and Rational Behaviour*. New York: Routledge, 2013.

Maas, Michael. Review of *Economy and Society in the Age of Justinian*, by Peter Sarris. *American Historical Review* 113, no. 2 (2008): 554–55.

MacCoull, Leslie S. B. *Dioscorus of Aphrodito: His Work and His World*. Berkeley: University of California Press, 1988.

Manning, J. G. *The Last Pharaohs: Egypt under the Ptolemies, 305–30 BC*. Princeton: Princeton University Press, 2009.

Manning, J. G., and Ian Morris. *The Ancient Economy: Evidence and Models*. Stanford: Stanford University Press, 2007.

Mathisen, Ralph. "*Adnotatio* and *petitio*." In *La pétition à Byzance*, edited by Denis Feissel and Jean Gascou, 23–32. Association des amis du Centre d'histoire et civilisation de Byzance, 2004.

Matthews, George. *The Royal General Farms in Eighteenth-Century France*. New York: Columbia University Press, 1958.

Mayerson, Philip. "*Mega Kankellon* and *Metron* in Late Receipt and Expenditure Accounts." *Bulletin of the American Society of Papyrologists* 43 (2006): 107–11.

Mazza, Roberta. *L'Archivio degli Apioni: Terra, lavoro e proprietà senatoria nell'Egitto tardoantico*. Bari: Edipuglia, 2001.

Mazza, Roberta. Review of Economy and Society in the Age of Justinian, by Peter Sarris. *Journal of Agrarian Change* 8, no. 1 (2008): 144–67.

McConnell, Ryan. "More Land, More Production, or More Taxes? Growth and the Apion Estate." *Bulletin of the American Society of Papyrologists* 53 (forthcoming).

Mirkovic, Miroslava. "*The Later Roman Colonate and Freedom*." *Transactions of the American Philosophical Society* 87, no. 2 (1997): 1–144.

Mirkovic, Miroslava. "Count Ammonios and Paying Taxes in the Name of Somebody Else in the Cadastre from Aphrodito." In *Proceedings of the 25th International Congress of Papyrology, Ann Arbor, July 29–August 4, 2007*, edited by Traianos Gagos, 565–72. Scholarly Publishing Office, University of Michigan Library, 2010.

Mokyr, Joel. *The Oxford Encyclopedia of Economic History*. Oxford: Oxford University Press, 2007.

Monson, Andrew. *From the Ptolemies to the Romans: Political and Economic Change in Egypt*. Cambridge: Cambridge University Press, 2012.

Montevecchi, O. "Il censimento romano d'Egitto: Preciziazioni." *Aevum* 50 (1970): 72–84.

Morris, Ian. "The Athenian Economy Twenty Years after *The Ancient Economy*." Review of *Athenian Economy and Society: A Banking Perspective*, by Edward E. Cohen. *Classical Philology* 89, no. 4 (1994): 351–66.

Oleson, John Peter. *Greek and Roman Mechanical Water-Lifting Devices: The History of a Technology*. Toronto: Springer, 1984.

Préaux, Claire. *L'économie Royale Des Lagides*. Bruxelles: Édition de la Fondation égyptologique Reine Élisabeth, 1939.

Rathbone, Dominic. *Economic Rationalism and Rural Society in Third-Century A.D. Egypt: The Heroninos Archive and the Appianus Estate*. Cambridge: Cambridge University Press, 1991.

Rémondon, R. "Les contradictions de la société égyptienne à l'époque byzantine." *Journal of Juristic Papyrology* 18 (1974): 17–32.

Rostovtzeff, Michael Ivanovitch. *The Social and Economic History of the Hellenistic World*. Oxford: Clarendon, 1941.

Rouillard, Germaine. *L'administration Civile de l'Égypte Byzantine*. Abbeville: P. Geuthner, 1928.

Rouillard, Germaine. *La vie rurale dans L'empire byzantin*. Paris: Librairie d'Amérique et d'Orient, 1953.

Rowlandson, Jane. "Crop Rotation and Rent Payment in Oxyrynchite Land Leases: Social and Economic Interpretations." In *Proceedings of the 20th International Congress of Papyrology*, edited by Adam Bülow-Jacobsen, 495–99. Museum Tusculanum Press, 1994.

Rowlandson, Jane. *Landowners and Tenants in Roman Egypt: The Social Relations of Agriculture in the Oxyrhynchite Nome*. Oxford: Clarendon, 1996.

Ruffini, Giovanni Roberto. "Social Networks in Byzantine Egypt." PhD diss., Columbia University, 2005.

Ruffini, Giovanni Roberto. "Risk and Administrative Pressure in the Archive of Dorotheos and Papnouthis." 137th Annual Meeting of the American Philological Association, Montréal, Québec, Canada January 8, 2006.

Ruffini, Giovanni Roberto. *Social Networks in Byzantine Egypt*. Cambridge: Cambridge University Press, 2008.

Ruffini, Giovanni Roberto. Review of *Economy and Society in the Age of Justinian*, by Peter Sarris. *Topoi* 16 (2009): 627–40.

Ruffini, Giovanni Roberto. *A Prosopography of Byzantine Aphrodito*. American Studies in Papyrology 50. Durham: American Society of Papyrologists, 2011.

Sarris, Peter. *Economy and Society in the Age of Justinian*. Cambridge: Cambridge University Press, 2006.

Sarris, Peter. "Social History and the Land." In *The Social History of Byzantium*, edited by John Haldon, 92–111. Oxford: Wiley-Blackwell, 2009.

Sarris, Peter. "The Early Byzantine Economy in Context: Aristocratic Property and Economic Growth Reconsidered." *Early Medieval Europe* 19 (2011): 255–84.

Schnebel, M. "An Agricultural Ledger in P. Bad. 95." *Journal of Egyptian Archaeology* 14 (1928): 34–45.

Shelton, John. "Artabs and Choenices." *Zeitschrift für Papyrologie und Epigraphik* 24 (1977): 55–67.

Shelton, John. "Two Notes on the Artab." *Zeitschrift für Papyrologie und Epigraphik* 42 (1981): 99–106.

Sirks, Boudewijn. "Reconsidering the Roman Colonate." *Zeitschrift der Savigny-Stiftung für Rechtsgeschichte: Romanistische Abteilung* 110 (1993): 331–69.

Ste. Croix, G. E. M. de. "Demosthenes' TIMHMA and the Athenian *Eisphora* in the Fourth Century B.C." *Classica et Mediaevalia* 14 (1953): 30–70.

Tate, G. *Les campagnes de la Syrie du Nord du IIe au VIIe siècle: Un exemple d'expansion démographique et économique dans les campagnes à la fin de l'Antiquité* Vol. 1. BAH 133. Libr. orientaliste P. Geuthner, 1992.

Thompson, Dorothy. "Economic Reforms in the Mid-Reign of Ptolemy Philadelphus." In *Ptolemy the Second Philadelphus and His World*, edited by Paul R. McKechnie and Philippe Guillaume, 27–38. Brill, 2008.

Thomsen, Rudi. *Eisphora: A Study of Direct Taxation in Ancient Athens*. København: Gyldendal, 1964.

Venticinque, Philip F. "Risk Management: Social Capital and Economic Strategies on Late Roman Estates in Oxyrhynchus." *Historia* 63, no. 4 (2014): 463–86.

Volbach, Wolfgang Fritz. *Elfenbeinarbeiten der Spätantike und des frühen Mittelalters: Bearbeitete Auflage*. Mainz, 1976.

Wallace, Sherman LeRoy. *Taxation in Egypt from Augustus to Diocletian*. Princeton: Princeton University Press, 1938.

Webber, Carolyn, and Aaron B. Wildavsky. *A History of Taxation and Expenditure in the Western World*. New York Simon and Schuster, 1986.

West, Louis C., and Allan Chester Johnson. *Currency in Roman and Byzantine Egypt*. Amsterdam: Hakkert, 1944.

Whittow, Mark. "The Late Roman / Early Byzantine Near East." In *The New Cambridge History of Islam*, edited by Chase F. Robinson *et al.*, 72–97. Cambridge: Cambridge University Press, 2010.

Youtie, Herbert C. "Publicans and Sinners." *Zeitschrift für Papyrologie und Epigraphik* 1 (1967): 1–20.

Zuckerman, C. *Du village à l'empire: Autour du registre fiscal d'Aphroditó (525–526)*. Paris: Association des Amis du Centre d'Histoire et Civilisation de Byzance, 2004.

Index

Greek Index

Printed and bound by CPI Group (UK) Ltd, Croydon, CR0 4YY

16/09/2026

14963491-0008